# The Three
# Agile Quality &
# Testing

*Achieving Balanced Results in Your Journey*
*Towards Agile Quality*

Robert Galen

Many of the designations used by manufacturers and sellers to distinguish their products are claimed as trademarks. Where those designations appear in this book, and the publisher was aware of the trademark claim, the designations have been printed with initial capital letters or all capitals.

The author and publisher have taken care in the preparation of this book, but make no expressed or implied warranty of any kind and assume no responsibility for errors of omission. No liability is assumed for incidental or consequential damages in connection with or arising out of the use of the information contained herein.

Cover Photo: *LochNess Sunset - Vertical*. Photographer – Michael Grab, Gravity Glue, licensed on September 11, 2014.

Print ISBN: 978-0-9885026-3-5
Electronic ISBN: 978-0-9885026-4-2

Printed in the United States

# Appreciations

## *Bob Galen thanks...*

I want to thank everyone that I've worked with on agile adoptions. No matter how well or how poorly you've done, I honor your efforts, intentions, and everything we've learned together. You've helped me to continually improve my agile coaching and servant leadership.

Specifically, I want to thank my ex-colleagues from iContact. Jeff Sutherland has talked for years about hyper-productive agile teams. It's never been clear to me what magic dust makes regular, high, or hyper performing agile teams. Is there a secret metric or a specific percentage increase in productivity? I honestly don't think so.

However, I do think agile done well has a particular 'feel' to it—in teams that are approaching "being Agile" in their mindset, daily activities, culture, and, more importantly, their results.

For 2 ½ years, I was fortunate and lucky enough to help build and coach just such a set of teams at iContact. In many ways, I wouldn't be the coach I am today without the opportunity to partner with this group. It was a distinct privilege to work with such fine "agilistas". From where I sit, we were very much...hyper-performing!

iContact was also the place where I first met my co-conspirator in developing many of the ideas within this book. I still remember the day when I interviewed Mary Thorn for a Director of Quality Assurance position. She was an absolute and wonderful find. She was knowledgeable, skilled, and very passionate. She was also a natural leader. In fact, she was almost too good during the interview! I actually recall having to "slow her down" when we spoke about early initiatives and challenges for her role.

Well, fast forward to today. Mary and I have become more than colleagues—we've become good friends. I admire Mary and believe that her contributions to this book make it all the more valuable – in the "real world". Thanks for keeping me grounded and honest Mary!

I want to once again thank my family -- my children have always been incredibly supportive of what I do, and my wife, Diane, has been a constant and tireless supporter. Diane, your patience and support, now and always, mean the world to me. Thank you for supporting what I love to do.

For those who know me, you know that Diane and I are fairly rabid pet lovers. During the time this book was evolving in my thinking, as well as writing it, we lost our beloved dog, Bentley. We love ALL of our animals dearly but Bentley held a special place in our hearts and our family. He was the quintessential protector of our home and, after we lost Foster, he was alone in these efforts. Bentley, our lives (and this book) are better for knowing you.

I'm quite positive he had a strong influence (and still does) on my agile coaching. We miss you Bent-meister!

Last but not least, I want to thank all of you for picking up this book, your interest in my thoughts, and for taking time out of your busy day to read this. I hope you find something of value within...to help you with your own journey.

Stay agile my friends...

## *Mary Thorn thanks...*

If you look up the definition of "mentor" it reads: "an experienced and trusted adviser". Bob Galen is that person to me. When I went on my interview at iContact with Bob, I knew from the beginning of the conversation that this was the person I wanted to work for. It proved nothing less than career altering for me.

From the day I stepped onto the iContact campus to today, Bob has been at my side leading me, coaching me, pushing me when I wouldn't, and/or couldn't, push myself, and teaching me that you can always improve. There is no way I will ever be able to thank him for the endless opportunities he has given me and I look forward to his continued guidance and mentorship in the future.

I also want to thank my partner, Kristi. The last 4 years has been tough on us with the birth of our 2 sons, me taking on 3 new jobs, and a side career on the testing and agile conference circuit. You have been the most loyal and supportive partner and I could have not done it without you.

## *We Both Thank...*

We both want to thank our colleagues and friends who reviewed and provided feedback for early versions of the book. Of particular note is TR Buskirk who spent considerable time giving us thoughtful and useful feedback.

Many thanks to ALL of you!

# Contents

# Forward

I've been consulting, teaching, and coaching software testing for the better part of two decades. I'm a software developer by training, so it would be fair for you to ask—why are you writing a book about agile testing?

First, many years ago I had the opportunity to move from a development leadership role to a testing leadership role. Believe me, it was quite a bit different, and much more challenging, than my development role. One of the things I decided early on was that I couldn't "lead" testers if I didn't understand them and the profession of testing.

Therefore, I became a student of software testing in all its forms. I didn't pretend that I understood it. Instead, I listened to my teams and learned. I attended courses, read quite a lot, and practiced testing. After a number of years, I felt that I'd earned sufficient chops to call myself an "honorary" tester and test leader. At this juncture, I feel I've got as good a handle on software quality and testing as I do on software development.

But beyond the understanding, I achieved a newfound and lasting respect for the art and science of software testing. I find it, and the people doing it, to be incredibly bright, focused, and valuable within software teams. But, not everyone holds that opinion – particularly in the agile community.

Therefore, my motivation in writing this book is three fold:

1. Software Testing is a profession AND a craft. It is as deep, rich, and challenging as software development. I want to honor the folks who have selected this professional path. In a word, Testers "Rock"!

2. If traditional testing was hard, agile testing is even harder—a moving target if you will. I find most traditional testers struggle to figure out the way. I hope to provide valuable insights and guidance for those embarking on this journey.

3. The agile methods are incredibly developer-centric in their origins. Out of 17 signatories to the agile manifesto, only one was a tester. So there is 'skew' in the methods and I feel compelled to rebalance things. Again, I hope this book contributes in a small way to adding to the quality and testing balance within your agile teams and organizations.

Another area where I envision influencing you is *continuous improvement*. I hope that the "Three Pillars" becomes a useful metaphor and model for you to think about, strategize, plan, and execute on your improvement plans.

In the only appendix to the book, you'll find a tool for assessing your maturity from a Three Pillars perspective. Please use it prudently and wisely.

I don't want you to use it for cross-team comparison, grading, and/or incentives. Instead, please use all of the concepts in the book to help guide your maturation during your agile adoption.

I often get asked about how long it takes to "become Agile". It's a fairly common question at conferences. Everyone is expecting an answer measured in months and, often, 6-18 seems to be an answer that many find palatable.

However, the real answer is years to never. I've been practicing the agile methods since 1997–1998, for over 15 years, yet I still find myself making mistakes, learning and growing in the methods.

Therefore, in true agile fashion, I hope this book inspires you now and into the future to try new things, learn, and grow as an agile practitioner. From my perspective, it's certainly a worthwhile endeavor!

## Format of this Book

In the first installment of the book, I'll be supplying six chapters that introduce and explore the Three Pillars at a high to moderate level. The target for the initial draft of the book is Quality Assurance and Testing Leadership; for VP's, Directors, Managers, Team Leads, Project Managers, etc. who are initiating and/or fine-tuning their agile adoption strategies from a testing and quality perspective.

I also feel the initial draft sets the tone for Quality and Testing Assessments that will leverage the Three Pillars as a model for assessment, reflection and improvement planning. To that end, we're providing a lightweight assessment framework tied to the pillars in the first installment.

But that's just the first installment. Mary and I plan on adding, what we're now calling, "Deep Dives", to the book as we move forward. For example:

- More details on **automation strategies** and mapping to the various tools;
- Exploring **Exploratory Testing** as a viable (and valuable) agile testing technique;
- The **3 Amigo's** and more details on just what **BDD** is trying to do; a hint: it's not "automation";
- Identifying and handling **Technical Test Debt;**
- Exploring the "power" of **Definition-of-Done** and Readiness Criteria, and
- Giving **Agile Metrics** its due with a much more detailed exploration of metrics patterns and anti-patterns.

Look for these additions after first publication. Mary and I will be iteratively adding content over the course of time. I'm not sure what the delivery mechanism for these will be. We might use Leanpub as a mechanism, or simply deliver PDF copies via the RGalen Consulting website.

Either way, if you acquire/purchase the first edition we'll work hard to make these available to you – so stay tuned via the website.

# Perspective

While I am the primary author of the book, Mary has been my key reviewer and has also contributed *Mary's Corner* stories in every chapter of the book. In fact, there are twenty-two of them. Mary helps to add a different perspective to my opinions and often, dare I say it, disagrees with me. She has also contributed Chapter 6 to the first edition and will be contributing more content over time.

### How to Read

I strongly suggest that you minimally read this introduction to start. Once you know where I'm going, then you can go wherever you want in the book. It's written to be read as a reference and in pieces.

Of course, I feel a "front to back" reading might provide the most value, but you should literally be able to pick it up, turn to a chapter, and glean some value from it. Or, at least, that is my hope.

*Chapter 1 – Introduction to the 3-Pillars*

The next three chapters provide a "moderately deeper dive" into each of the pillars:

*Chapter 2, Pillar 1 – Automation and Tools*
*Chapter 3, Pillar 2 – Software Testing*
*Chapter 4, Pillar 3 – Team Practices*

Next, I wanted to provide some guidance around leveraging the pillars in your agile adoption. These chapters are more focused towards managing and leading from a Three Pillars (and Agile) point of view.

*Chapter 5, 3-Pillars Transformation Strategies*
*Chapter 6, Role of the QA Manager in Agile Teams*

Finally, I felt compelled to provide some sort of "assessment" guidance for this initial draft of the book.

*Appendix A, 3-Pillars Assessment Tool!*

## And Finally, Value?

Thank you again for picking up the book. In the end, we hope you find some value in these pages and it helps you and your teams achieve the wonderful promise of 'Agile' done well.

Stay agile my (our) Friends!

Bob Galen
Spring 2015
Cary, NC

Mary Thorn
Spring 2015
Raleigh, NC

# Chapter 1 – Three Pillars:

# Introduction & Foundations

A few years ago I entered an organization to do some agile focused coaching and training. From the outside looking in, it was a fairly mature agile organization. They had internal coaches in place, had implemented Scrum, and had also been leveraging extreme programming technical practices for a couple of years. They appeared to be fairly committed to and rigorous in their application of the methods.

It was a global financial firm that delivered their IT projects via highly distributed teams. There were a wide variety of tools in place, both for Application Lifecycle Management (ALM), software development, and software testing support. In my first few days, everything I encountered, while albeit in superficial detail, just felt like a mature agile organization and I was pleasantly surprised. Heck, I was impressed!

For the purposes of this introduction, my observations will shift to be quality, testing, and tester centric.

## *Too Narrow a Focus*

One of the things I noticed is that the firm had gone "all in" on Behavior-Driven Development (BDD) leveraging Cucumber as the primary tooling framework. They had invited in several consultants to teach courses to many of their Scrum teams and everyone got "test infected"[1]. Teams were literally creating thousands of BDD level automated tests in conjunction with delivering their software. From their perspective, there was incredible energy and enthusiasm. Everyone contributed tests while measuring the number of increasing Cucumber tests on a daily basis.

---

[1] To use a term coined by Elizabeth Hendrickson – http://testobsessed.com/

However, a few days into my coaching, I was invited to a backlog refinement session where a team was writing and developing their user stories. What I expected was to simply be an observer. What actually happened is that I quickly realized the team didn't know how to write a solid user story. They could barely write one at all. On their request, I ended up delivering an ad-hoc user story writing class for them. Afterwards, the team was incredibly appreciative as they started to understand the important place that solid story writing held in the agile development lifecycle.

Over the next few days, I realized something very important. The organization was at two levels when it came to their agile quality and testing practices. Either they were <u>all in</u>, or they were <u>unaware of, or under-practicing</u> specific techniques. For example, they were all in on BDD and writing automated Cucumber tests and on Continuous Integration; however, they struggled mightily with simply writing user stories and, literally, had no clear or consistent Definition-of –Done or DoD.

This "see-saw" effect of focusing on a hand-full of practices was doing them a disservice. Why? Because it's actually the interplay across practices that largely influences the effectiveness of your agile testing and the product impact of your quality practices. I prepared a view for them to illustrate the balance that, I believe, is critical in your agile quality practices. I called it, "<u>The Three Pillars of Agile Quality and Testing</u>", and began using it to coach a much more nuanced, broad, and deep approach for their teams.

While this is more of a strategic play with a longer-term focus, the discussions and changes that the model drove had an immediate impact on the organization at all levels. I want to share the "Pillars" in this book with the hope that it will also help your agile quality strategy development.

In fact, I want to introduce my "partner in crime" at this point. Mary Thorn and I have both experienced the above scenario in multiple agile coaching engagements. We've seen the effect that imbalanced or non-existent agile test strategies do to organizations adopting agility. In a word, it's not pretty! Trying to bring some rigor to agile testing and quality strategies is our motivation for the book and we'll be sharing some hard-fought lessons with you along the way.

While I'm the primary author for the book, Mary will be weighing in more than occasionally with what we'll be calling "**Mary's Corner**". Here, she will share stories and examples from her experience(s) that complement the Three Pillars. Believe it or not, Mary will not always agree with me, so you'll often get some contrasting opinions and advice. Our hope is that book will be that much better for it.

## *The Three Pillars of Agile Quality and Testing*

The driving force behind creating the Three Pillars is organizational quality imbalance. As I travel in my coaching and consulting, I see imbalanced initiatives again and again. Often, as in the case with my introductory story, technology or tooling is an initial push, or focus, but even then not completely in a balanced fashion. For example, not focusing on Continuous Integration in parallel with automation.

In the beginning it was unclear to me how to create a model that would help my clients and the agile community at-large. Then, after a while, I witnessed enough repeated patterns that I came upon the following three critical areas or 'Pillars'. Here I categorized crucial tactics, strategies, and techniques that help agile teams create a broad and deep supportive structure towards their product quality and testing activities:

*(Note: we'll explore all of the ideas mentioned in the other pillars below in each associated chapter...so please be patient.)*

1. **Development and Test Automation:** This pillar is the technology-side of quality and testing and is not simply focused towards testing and testers. It includes tooling, execution of the Automation Test Pyramid, Continuous Integration, deep use of Extreme Programming technical practices, and support for ALM distributed collaboration tools.

   It's often the place where organizations gravitate towards first—probably because of our general affinity towards tools and technology solving all of our challenges. An important way to think about this pillar is that it is foundational, in that the other two pillars are built on top of the tooling. And often, organizations underestimate the importance, initial cost, and ongoing costs, to maintain foundational agility in this pillar. Investment and focus is an ongoing challenge here (*see Mary's Corner below*).

Finally, this pillar is not centric to the testing function or group. While it includes test tooling and automation, it inherently includes ALL tooling related to product development across the entire agile organization. It provides much of the "glue" in cross-connecting tools and automation towards efficiency and quality.

2. **Software Testing:**  This pillar is focused towards the profession of testing. Towards solid testing practices, not simply agile testing practices, but leveraging the teams' past testing experience, skills, techniques, and tools. This is the place where agile teams move from a trivial view to software testing, which only looks at TDD, ATDD, and developer-based testing, towards a more holistic view of agile quality and testing.

   It's a pillar where the functional and non-functional testing breadth and depth is embraced. It's also where exploratory testing is understood and practiced as a viable testing technique. It's where non-functional testings' breadth and requirements are fully understood and applied to meet business and domain needs, including: performance, load, security, and customer usability testing.

   By definition, this is where testing strategy resides, where planning and governance sits, and where broad reporting is performed. To be clear, I'm not talking about traditional testing with all of its process-focus and gatekeeper mindset. Instead, I'm talking about effective professional testing, broadly and deeply applied within agile contexts.

3. **Cross Functional Team Practices:**  Finally, this pillar is focused towards cross-team collaboration, team-based standards, quality attitudes, agile mindsets, and, most importantly, towards building things right. Consider this the soft skills area of the Three Pillars, where direction is provided for

how each team will operate. You could also consider them "rules of engagement".

For example, this is the place where good old-fashioned "reviews" are valued. This would include pairing across ALL team members, but also slightly more formal reviews of architecture, design, code, and test cases. It's a place where inspection is valued and performed rigorously as established by the teams' Definition-of-Done. It's also where refactoring of the code base and, keeping it "well kept", is of major importance.

Speaking of DoD, this is the pillar where cross-team physical constraints, conventions, and agreements are established. But, more importantly than creating them, it's where the team makes commitments to consistency and actually "holding to" their agreements. These agreements (or promises) include those to the customer for delivering high-value, high-quality, and high-impact features that truly solve their problems.

I'm sure many readers will have differing opinions regarding the Three Pillars. Why three for example, why not four, or five? Or why was this practice placed here versus there? Or, you've forgotten "this" – does that mean it isn't important?

I've seen this same type of over analysis occur in the 4 Quadrants of Agile Testing that Lisa Crispin and Janet Gregory have shared in their book *Agile Testing*. An important point to emphasize about the Three Pillars is to not get too hung up on the model. It's not intended to constrain you or to serve as the definitive view of agile testing. It's simply a model.

Ultimately my intent is to get you thinking about your agile testing, and to help guide you towards more balanced strategies. Please don't take it too seriously. It's a thinking tool and a starting point. Yes, I think it's sound, but I want you to make it context-based and adapt it to your context.

## Mary's Corner

*Bob, I don't think you've emphasized enough how important it is to establish a solid Test Automation framework as part of every agile adoption effort. Yes, there needs to be balance across the Three Pillars. But there also needs to be a foundation in technology-based infrastructure in order to truly perform as an agile organization.*

*This would include initial and ongoing investments in:*

- *Automation infrastructure*
- *Test Automation*
- *Test environments (virtualization, data, production-level mirrors)*
- *Continuous Integration and/or Continuous Deployment*
- *Development Support tooling*
- *Test Support tooling*

*Too many firms trivialize these investments and are unwilling to pay for the initial, ramp-up costs and the ongoing maintenance costs (as well as the trade-offs between this sort of investment vs. customer-facing features).*

*You don't need to have all of this overnight, BUT you need to be relentless in the pursuit of technical infrastructure support.*

*Figure 1* is an overview of the types of activity and focus within each pillar. This is a high-level view and there are important nuances that are missing—mostly due to a lack of space. That's why we'll be drilling into each of these pillars later on in subsequent chapters.

Figure 1, High-level View of the Three Pillars

## *The Foundations of the Pillars*

There are some key concepts that permeate through the model and across the Three Pillars. They are the first concepts that are crosscutting in nature—serving as a foundation. But they're also things that, at least in my estimation, are ongoing goals rather than things you achieve overnight. Instead, you should be constantly focusing on, investing in, talking about, and evolving them within your agile transformation.

I want to explore each one in a bit of detail, because frankly they are *that* important.

## Whole-Team Ownership

I encounter many, many teams in my agile coaching. I also interact with numerous coaches. So, my sample size in this case is relatively large. We all talk about breaking down functional silos when forming and operating within agile teams – particularly the "wall between" developers and testers. However, the reality is that in most agile organizations today, while everyone tries to be a team, functional silos are still alive and well.

As you move into implementation of the Three Pillars, a constant emphasis needs to be placed on the team in your formation of teams, planning, and in your day-to-day conversations. You have to move from "development" plus "testing" to the "team" in everything you say and do.

One of my key measures of whether you're operating as a team is: how actively, willingly, and happily the developers dive into testing during a sprint. If you have this sort of behavior, where they view their jobs beyond their functional silo of writing code, then you might be on the cusp of true whole-team ownership.

I've found that this is mostly a led practice. That is, the leadership team within the organization de-emphasizes each functional silo and reemphasizes the whole-team view. Not only do they do that within their teams, but they also do it by creating a leadership partnership across their own functional silos. This makes it clear to their teams that cross-functional team engagement is now the new operational imperative.

## Mary's Corner

*Bob, whole-team ownership is a tricky one. From a leadership perspective when I have come into organizations, there is always a consensus that "Yes" each Scrum team owns quality. However, when the rubber meets the road and there is a severity-one issue post-production, who is the first one blamed? Inevitably the testers!*

*At that point, I often realize whom within the organization, and who on the Scrum teams, believes in whole team quality. What I try to do then is to create a partnership with the Scrum Master, the Product Owner and*

*the Development managers on every Scrum team. When we have a
severity-one issue, I ask that the Scrum team hold a retrospective just on
that issue.*

*I often coach senior leadership to realize and understand that QA cannot
always guarantee quality and that we cannot find every bug.*

*We hope that we shine a light on the worst issues and then the business
can make risk-based decisions as to whether or not to release the
software. But, quality is built in from the grooming sessions, to the
implementation, and then, to the testing. At any point, one of those things
could break down and it is the <u>responsibility of the team</u> to hold each
other accountable.*

---

## Knowing the Right Thing to Build and Building it Right

This should become the mission statement across everyone who has
"QA or Testing" in his or her role descriptions. Clearly the "build it right"
alludes to the professionalism, craftsmanship, and integrity of the entire
team. When they attack user stories, do they do a complete job without
cutting corners? Are the stories well and thoughtfully designed? Are
they crafted according to the teams' Definition-of-Done? And is all of
this done consistently – story after story? Testers can make such a
difference by becoming <u>quality champions</u> within their teams, as well
as, helping to keep everyone focused on these goals.

But, that's sort of a "back of the line" responsibility—checking and
verifying.

What about assuring that the team is building something that will
actually solve the customers' problems, perhaps going beyond what
they asked for, but providing what they truly need. This is another area
of focus for the tester in agile teams. I sometimes call it – moving to the
front of the line. Being more directly involved with the customer and
also helping to define and refine user stories so that the resulting
functionality truly provides value to and delights the customer.

At the end of the day, we want our customers to be raving fans of our
teams. Right?

## Healthy Agile Metrics

Several times in the book I will explore what "healthy" agile metrics look like. You see some discussion in the Pillar 2 and Strategy chapters. But beyond that, I want you to be constantly vigilant in your metrics.

There are two primary considerations:

1. **Agile Metrics are Different!** When you begin your agile transformation, you want to move from functional metrics to team-based metrics. It's a fundamental shift that is incredibly important, but far too many organizations ignore and/or resist it.
2. **Avoid Metrics Dysfunction!** This has little to do with "agile" and much more to do with defining sound metrics. We've had a habit in our industry of measuring the wrong things. Robert Austin wrote a very good book that explored *Metrics Dysfunction* [2]and the inherent organizational challenges it creates.

I want you to view your shift towards agility as a place to start fresh with what you measure, how you measure, and how you and your team's react to the measures. Please keep this in the back of your minds as you instantiate your agile teams and begin to instill a Three Pillars view towards your quality and testing.

## Mary's Corner

*Bob, this topic alone keeps me employed. Can we just change the world to ask the question, "What does 'good' look like for your organization?" and, "Are your customers happy?"*

*For the past five years, I have been in more meetings about creating better metrics for agile teams then the previous ten years combined. At the end of the day, it's difficult for those above to trust the team, that 30*

---

[2] Robert Austin published the book: *Measuring and Managing Performance in Organizations* in 1996. It's still one of the best books that explore metrics. It starts from the perspective of examining metrics dysfunction and then explores the factors highlighting more healthy measures.

*points is their velocity, that 60% might be good enough for their code coverage, that 80% of their regression test suite is automated.*

*They want more numbers and, to be honest, they just want their waterfall metrics. It made them feel warm and cozy because you had objective measures. If this was an easy problem to solve, there would be books written on it and people would be happy with "agile metrics". The problem is, that it is not easy, and what is important to one organization, won't be important for the next.*

*What I like about the Three Pillars is that it is my scorecard, my metrics to say, this is what I think "Good Agile Testing" looks like.*

---

## An Aside: Classic Measurement Dysfunctions

Just to illustrate a couple of examples of metrics dysfunction, here are two 'classic' examples:

- *If you measure and compensate/reward developers by the Lines of Code they produce, you will get...LOTS of lines of code, but might miss value, design, craft, quality, maintainability, etc.*
- *If you measure and compensate/reward testers by the Number of Tests (coverage) they run, you will get...LOTS of tests running over and over, but missing risk, intentionality, new tests, exploration, thoughtful coverage, etc.*

---

## Steering

In the foundation I also identify the notion of Agile Centers of Excellence or Communities of Practice. From my perspective, both of these are mechanisms for 'steering' your agile adoption and transformation. The emphasis here is on the steering of things.

As far as steering, I've often found two common problems. First, organizations do too little to no steering of their adoptions. Sure they might pull a committee together that reads a few books and meet every two weeks, but that isn't steering from my point of view. And it's largely uninformed. Therefore, the steering not only needs to occur, but it needs to be led by experienced agile coaches.

Many organizations are reluctant to seek external, expert advice. Sometimes it's budgetary constraints, but in my experience, it's more often a reluctance to ask for help, preferring to implement agility on their own. Often you hear the mantra of – "Agile" is so simple, of course we can do it.

The second key problem is that the quality and testing organization is rarely an equal partner in the agile transformation. Instead, they are often along for the ride with the technology or development organizations that drive the majority of the agile strategies.

While I don't have a problem with development doing some of it, the Three Pillars is truly predicated on their being a whole-team – not only at the agile team level, but also at the leadership team level. That means that QA and test leadership need to be an integral part of guiding and steering the organizations evolution.

Key areas that come to mind as part of this steering include:

1. Test Automation and CI or CD
2. Test Environments
3. Process Artifacts
4. Definition of Done
5. Measures
6. Agile Testing Practices
7. Continuous Improvement
8. Customer Engagement

## Crosscutting Concerns

You'll notice at the base of the Three Pillars, a foundational layer that captures crosscutting concerns that are central to the effective balance of the pillars. For example, the mantra of:

> *Responsibly building the right things and building them right...*

Is central to the quality proposition that is inherent in high-performance agile teams. The teams need to focus first on the client challenges, interact with them, and provide solutions that appropriately meet those needs. In addition, those solutions need to be sound, well crafted, and of high quality. They simply need to <u>work</u>.

## *Crosscutting Strategies*

Beyond the individual pillars, the value resides in crosscutting concerns. Let's go back to the original story to help make this point. My client was advanced in BDD practices, but struggling with user story writing, or even understanding "the point of" the user story. Here they should have made the following cross-pillar connections:

- In Pillar #1 – Behavior-driven Development (BDD) and Acceptance Test-driven Development (ATDD) are mostly technical practices. They focus on articulating user story acceptance testing in such a way as to make them automatable via a variety of open source tooling. Unfortunately, they have an underlying assumption that you understand story development, and are <u>connecting</u> the acceptance test <u>to</u> the customers' needs and value. It's also important to understand that these are NOT functionally focused automated tests.

- In Pillar #2 – One thing I didn't mention in the story, was that every team had a different view towards what a story should look like, as well as, the "rules" for writing effective stories. There were no norms, consistency guidance, or even solid examples. A focus on the <u>software testing</u> aspects of Pillar 2 would have established these practices, which would have helped their teams not only do a better job, but raise impediments if some teams weren't adhering to the "rules".

- **In Pillar #3** – An important aspect of the user story that this organization failed to realize was the conversation-part of the story. If you reference the *3-C's* [3] of effective story writing as a model, one of the C's is having a conversation, or collaborating, around the story. It's the most important 'C' if you ask me. It's where the *"3 Amigo's" of the story* [4] (the Developer(s), the Tester(s), and the Product Owner(s) get together and leverage the story to create conversations that surround what customer problem are they trying to solve.

Do you see the pattern in this case?

You can't effectively manage to deliver on agile quality practices without crosscutting the concerns. In this case, effective use of user stories and standards, plus BDD and automation, as well as, the conversations are needed to effectively cross all Three Pillars.

It requires a strategic balance in order to implement any one of the practices properly.

As you and I explore each of the pillars, I'll try to continuously "connect the dots" across them. However, I hope that you start doing that on your own as well.

**Now onto the Three Pillars...**

---

[3] I believe the 3-C's were coined by Ron Jefferies about the characteristics of User Stories. The C's are:
1. C – Card (front of card; As a, I want, So that)
2. C – Confirmation (confirmation or acceptance tests)
3. C – Conversation (collaboration)
It's often said that the Conversation is the most important C.
[4] I explore the 3-Amigo's notion in much more detail in Chapter 4 as we dive into Pillar 3.

# Chapter 2 – Pillar #1:

# Development & Test Automation

Pillar 1 is the technically focused pillar and the one that agile organizations are usually quite comfortable discussing – at least at a high level. It's where automation, in general, is located. Terms like Continuous Integration, Continuous Deployment, Cucumber, *TDD, ATDD, BDD*[5], virtualization, and DevOps are actively discussed and implemented here.

But, beyond the more software development centric tooling, the Agile Lifecycle Management tooling typically resides here as well. This could include a robust *ALM*[6] tool such as Rally or VersionOne, or it could include a simple collection of tools like Jira Agile, a Wiki, and Google Apps. Information radiators, dashboards, and reporting are also part of this pillar.

I want to drill into a specific set of attributes and practices within the pillar in this chapter. Clearly, there won't be time to explore every technical tool or technique, however, I hope to explore this pillar

---

[5] I sometimes refer these as the DD's.
- TDD – is Test-Driven Development. Think of it as unit tests and testing. The tools here are language and technology stack dependent. Typically, the xUnit framework is the default tool, with junit, nunit, and phpunit common variants.
- ATDD – is Acceptance Test-Driven Development. These are tied to user story acceptance tests and are connected to tools such as Test Robot or FitNesse.
- BDD – is Behavior-Driven Development. Again, there is a specific format for the test writing here: Given-When-Then. It is also coupled to Cucumber and several other tools that try to articulate the tests in a human interaction / behavior format.

[6] ALM can either refer to Application Lifecycle Management or Agile Lifecycle Management. In the context of this article, I'm referring to the latter.

sufficiently for you to expand your thinking when it comes to these tools and practices within your agile testing strategies.

*Figure 2* provides an overview of the key focus factors for Pillar 1.

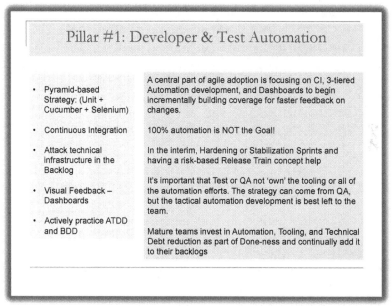

Figure 2, Pillar #1 - Development & Test Automation

Now I would like to start diving into more of the specific practices and/or tactics that reside within this pillar.

## Continuous Integration and/or Continuous Deployment

"Build as often as possible" was an early mantra of the agile methods. The Extreme Programming folks use the term *Continuous Integration or CI* to identify the practice. Early on, the frequency wasn't all that often, as the application architectures and tooling weren't designed for ultra-frequent integration builds and testing.

But then, the open source community began to introduce tools that focused on Continuous Integration or CI. One of the early tools of note was Cruise Control. It provided the necessary infrastructure to setup an environment that could run frequent builds and then run test sets against them. It also had some simple dashboards for teams to understand build quality, failures – blocks, and facilitated progress in repairing build issues.

From a Three Pillars perspective, the less important decision is what CI tool you use. There are many on the market, both open source and commercial, to choose from. The more important point is that you invest and focus on CI as a foundational component within your agile teams. The key agile benefit is that it provides a continuous feedback loop for checking integration and overall application stability and integrity.

## *Continuous Integration – Top 5 Mistakes*

It might be useful to share the top five anti-patterns related to Continuous Integration that I often see when coaching agile teams. Clearly, my sample size is small, but I do think the patterns are more pervasive than my experience indicates. You might want to construct your CI strategy with some of these in mind:

1. Organizations don't focus on CI in their agile adoption strategies. Instead, they remain hopeful that development-centric tooling such as Continuous Integration will simply and naturally emerge from the self-directed teams themselves.
2. Organizations only invest in the start-up of their CI effort, viewing it as a short-term investment. They lack the planning foresight for longer term, ongoing investments. This is often exacerbated in larger-scale organizations.
3. Organizations often forget that automation is an integral part of CI viability and don't focus on it at all; this refers to all levels of application automation and test automation infrastructure.
4. Transparent information is a hallmark of mature agility. However, many organizations forget to aggressively create effective dashboards and information radiators triggered from their CI frameworks. A variant of this mistake is paying attention to too many metrics or indicators.
5. Organizations don't integrate with Pillar 3, on "stop-the-line", root cause analysis, and/or other continuous improvement activities interrelated to continuous integration. They simply miss the fact that Continuous Integration is a "whole team" activity.

## *From an Agile Testing Perspective*

The important part, from a tester's perspective, is to partner with the Continuous Integration frameworks and tooling to truly integrate all types of testing tools, results reporting, and automation. Don't create another system and don't look at it as a testing activity. It's a whole-team activity and you'll want to partner with your development and operations colleagues to create an expansive system that accommodates all of the team's needs – including those supporting functional, non-functional, manual, and automated testing.

To put it succinctly, you need to aggressively <u>care about and engage with</u> your organizations Continuous Integration efforts.

## Mary's Corner

*Bob, it is interesting to me how many companies I have walked into that had automation but the tests were running only on their QA desktops. The QA engineers had been asking for an environment, virtual machine, or even a floating laptop, something to run their test in, but upper management would not fund the initiative.*

*This often perplexed me, because at the end of the day if the tests are not run on a schedule, in an integrated environment, what value do they provide?*

*As a QA leader, I often find myself walking into organizations and reworking their entire CI process so that QA can integrate their automated tests. A key point here is when hiring QA leadership; ask them about Continuous Integration and Continuous Deployment. If they can explain their build/deploy/test/release process, then you know this person at least understands this important part of effective test automation within agile contexts.*

## *The Agile Test Automation Pyramid*

The next practice is implementing an effective strategy for your overall automation development. It was Mike Cohn who established the initial model of a pyramid view towards contrasting traditional and then agile test automation. This model is fairly widely known and accepted as the *Agile Test Automation Pyramid*[7].

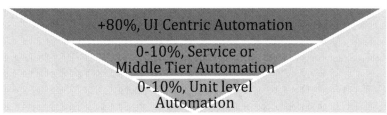

Figure 3, Traditional Test Automation Pyramid

In the traditional view, most if not all of the effort, over 80%, is focused towards developing UI-centric automated functional tests that explored the application via the GUI. There might be a few lower-level tests or unit tests, but teams mostly stay at the upper tier.

Why?

For several reasons, but first and foremost, the testers were the ones primarily writing the automation and, therefore, their comfort zone was towards functional testing. It didn't help that the majority of the automated testing tools were focused towards the functional UI as well.

Developers operated in the service and unit tiers and typically didn't invest much of their time in developing automated tests. There was little value in it from their perspective, especially when they were often being driven to deliver the features by prescribed dates.

However this strategy is flawed. It is inherently unstable, brittle and, because the application (UI) changes the automation, it is nearly always impacted. Therefore, one problem is automation instability and the high cost of ongoing maintenance. Another problem is that it doesn't engage

---

[7] There is not a good reference for the original proposed idea. In my research, it appears to pre-date 2008 and a conference presentation surrounding it. You can see Mike referencing the idea here in another context.

the entire team. Instead, the testers, who usually comprise a minor portion of the team, typically develop it. Quite often they are also consumed with manual testing, which limits the time they can spend developing and maintaining the automation.

The agile test automation pyramid is a strategy that attempts to turn all of this literally around.

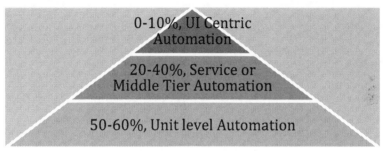

Figure 4, Agile Test Automation Pyramid

## Turning Things Around

The first change is to take a whole-team view. Instead of the testers being responsible for testing and writing all of the test automation, it becomes a whole-team responsibility. The developers take most of the ownership for unit-level automation at the base of the pyramid, but testers can operate there as well. The upper tier focuses on limited UI-centric automation. Usually, these are longer running, core customer usage workflows that are best implemented at this level.

The testers typically operate on these, but please remember that there are very few tests within this tier. Also, remember that the developers can operate here too. The two layers are met by middle-tier automation. This is often the domain of the open source ATDD/BDD tools, such as: FitNesse, Cucumber, JBehave, Robot Framework, and some others. Many team members can and do contribute at the middle-tier depending on their comfort and skill levels.

One thing to note, is that traditional automation was often a one-tool operation, with Mercury/HP commercial tooling (Quick Test Professional or, Unified Functional Testing - UFT), leading that space. The agile approach is tool agnostic, but also selects tools that are appropriate for each layer. Therefor, no "one-size fits all" thinking is allowed.

For example, as of this writing, these are common tools leveraged at each of the three tiers:

1. **UI tier:** Selenium, Watir, or traditional UFT
2. **Middle tier:** FitNesse, Robot Framework, JBehave, and Cucumber
3. **Unit tier:** xUnit family variants for example JUnit or NUnit for Java and .Net respectively

The other consideration is that there are extensions to several of these. For example, both Robot Framework and Cucumber have Selenium plug-ins so that they can drive the UI, as well as, the middle tier. This implies that the middle tier tooling, and automated tests for that matter, can extend or blend into the lower and upper tiers.

## *Advantages?*

The advantages of this approach mirror the disadvantages of the traditional approaches. First and foremost, if you take a whole-team approach, you now have automation work crossing every team member—so your capacity is increased. You also get better automation designs and improved testability because developers are weighing in.

Another important benefit is maintenance. It becomes a team-wide responsibility to keep up with automation maintenance, both the infrastructure and the tests, as the team is developing functional user stories. I personally like to make it part of the organizational and teams' Definition-of-Done, for consistency and rigor in maintaining automation assets.

For example, I would consider a story not to be "done" unless all of the automation associated with it, new and old, is working correctly (i.e. the tests pass). The *Scaled Agile Framework* [8](SAFe) actually recommends this view as a part of the framework.

---

[8] The Scaled Agile Framework or SAFe is becoming a very popular way to view agile scaling. You can review the framework here – www.scaledagile.com

An advantage that I didn't emphasize in the traditional case is automation coverage. One could argue that automation from the UI down was a limited exercise. There was always back-end functionality and business logic that was incredibly hard to reach via the automation. Internal infrastructure was nearly impossible to exercise / test via automation as well. In a multi-tiered approach, you should be able to reach any behavior or functionality that the team deems to have value in automating.

## Two Final Cautions

I've found it surprising, but true, that many developers don't really understand how to write effective unit tests – especially when you expect those tests to be part of a cohesive automation whole. Partnering with testers can help immensely when designing unit tests, even if the testers can't program in the language du jour. I've also found that training can really be a force multiplier here. That would include a 3-4-5 day class focused on OO design skills, patterns, refactoring, and TDD. That combination can be incredibly helpful in creating a baseline of solid skills across your entire team.

And a final caution – don't try to automate everything! The strategy or business case for 100% automation is nonsense. I'm usually against setting any sort of "magic number" when establishing goals for automation levels of coverage. Rather, ask the team to look at each user story and determine the appropriate level of unit, middle-tier, and UI tests in order to adequately cover it compared to its complexity and value. Then, implement those tests as part of your done-ness criteria. This leads to every story having a different level, which is determined by the team. Point being—trust your teams to determine the right balance between automation and other relevant forms of testing.

## Mary's Corner

*Bob, it is not that I disagree with you that you should not automate everything, I agree 100% with that—pun intended. However, I think you should automate the most used parts of the application, the most defect prone parts, and the interfaces or integration points. In those areas though I would like to have <u>at least 70%</u> or greater automated (includes unit, integration and system) tests.*

*I also want to make another point...*

*I have found that if you pick an automation tool that is not in the same language of the application that the developers are coding in, it's much harder for the whole-team ownership to take place. Even though Ruby is easier to pick up than Java or C# for most testers, implementing an automation tool in Ruby will not be as successful if most of the developers are C# programmers.*

*I have seen it work, but only when the culture from top down is that quality is owned by the whole team. If you are a QA leader and just beginning to push the notion that quality is owned by the whole team, do yourself a favor and pick an automation tool in the same language stack that the application is built in, it will save you a good deal of frustration.*

## *From an Agile Testing Perspective*

I like to think of the agile automation pyramid as THE model for automated testing strategy within the agile organization. While the execution of the triangle is a whole-team activity, I believe the QA and Test team leaders, as well as, the testing community should spearhead the automation strategies themselves.

This involves getting seasoned and experienced test leaders and automation architects to lead efforts that will evangelize the strategy and approach. They also should guide their organizations towards effective tools selection. Often, having a tooling "bake-off" is an effective way to garner whole team awareness, interest, and feedback in the selection process.

## Mary's Corner

*Here's a short story about not having the right test leader (architect) in place. A couple of years ago, I interviewed for a small startup company for a QA Manager role. This company had never had QA leadership - only strong development leadership. They wanted a QA manager to come in and create a cohesive test automation framework, as they had invested a lot in Continuous Integration, but did not have any test automation running.*

*I really wanted this job! It was a great company and had a great culture. Unfortunately, things did not work out and I was unable to pursue the opportunity.*

*Six months later they still had not filled the position and decided to hire a development manager to lead this effort. Then, six months later, I received a call from two of the testers that had interviewed me asking for advice on how to get the test automation framework up and working. I gave them some advice and did not hear from them again until almost a year later.*

*This time they called me – totally defeated. They told me that they have tried everything, but the manager just did not get it. He didn't understand QA, nor, did he understand test automation and the value it can deliver – even though he realized that something was needed. I asked them to talk to their manager once again, with more ammunition that I gave them, and if that did not work, to talk to his manager.*

*Two weeks later they called me back to ask me if I had any available opportunities at my current company. When I asked them what happened, they told me they took my advice, talked to their boss, and then talked to his boss. The company finally admitted that they intentionally hired a development manager to lead the automation effort, and that would be their strategy moving forward as well. This to me was sad. They had so much potential. But, back to Bob's point, they had no test architect leading the efforts to evangelize the strategy, approach and to guide their organizations towards <u>an effective</u> test automation framework.*

## A Real World Example

In *Figure 5*, you see an example of our automation implementation at iContact. I've literally plucked this snapshot from a real-time status wiki page. It was where we stood in actual test counts in mid-2012.

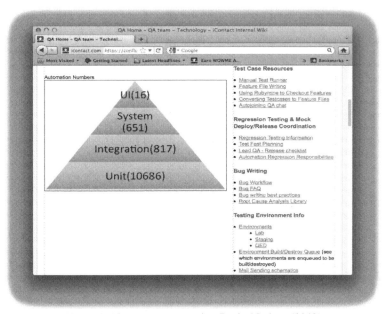

Figure 5, iContact Automation Pyramid circa (2012)

In our case, we leveraged a 3-tier model, but we differentiated between system-level and integration-level tests in the *middle tier[9]*.

Our view was that integration-level tests were tests implemented in Cucumber, our tool choice in the middle tier, but they were focused more towards unit-level testing. Another way of saying it is that these were larger-scale unit tests. Our system-layer tests were true middle tier tests that were focused more on functional behavior. Of course, there was a *fuzzy line* between the two.

I've found this is often the case in real world projects where the pyramid boundaries are not always clearly cut. In our case, we defined

---

[9] In other words, interpret this as: out of a total of 12,170 automated tests, we had 10,686 unit-level, 1468 middle-tier, and 16 UI-level automated tests. Or 87%, 12%, and less than 1% respectively. Just as a specific real world example.

categories that worked for us, and allowed us to report on execution at the various layers.

Another important point is that everything below the UI level tests were intended to be run on a code check-in basis. When every developer performed a check-in, approximately 12k tests would be run to provide feedback as part of our Continuous Integration tooling and virtualization environments. Therefore, these tests needed to be developed and scaled with performance in mind.

We were constantly tweaking our tests to bring the execution time within reasonable constraints for our team. Usually, are targets were less than 5 minutes for our unit and integration tests, and less than an hour for our system level tests. This was based on our commitment to run as many tests as possible on finely grained code chunks so that we could get broad degrees real-time feedback.

It was hard work to keep it tight, but definitely well worth the efforts.

## Mary's Corner

*When I was hired at iContact, I was excited about the opportunity to work with a leading-edge automaton framework called Cucumber. The first week on the job was very interesting; I had several of the QA Engineers talk to me about all these new tools that they wanted to replace Cucumber with. Granted, they had just implemented Selenium and failed. They had built a Selenium framework from scratch for 6 months, but only had coded 16 tests. They then went to Cucumber and already had 200-300 tests in about 4 weeks. So, it was difficult for me to imagine why they would want to switch again.*

*When I finally was able to get to the root of the issue, the trouble was they had implemented a headless browser called 'Celerity' and were having major problems with it. First, they were never able to capture screen shots when tests failed and, the debug time took forever. Celerity, at the time, was also not being maintained in the open source community and, therefore, the bugs that were found were not getting fixed. Lastly, it was not as fast as we had hoped it would be. The solution they were proposing was to switch to Watir or Selenium Webdriver[10] – both alternative, open source UI automation tools.*

*After discussing this situation with Bob, he suggested a tools bake-off. We came up with the acceptance criteria of what we needed the tools to do and created two stories – one for Watir and another for Selenium. Next, we had all three of our automation engineer's swarm on the Watir story. Once completed, they then moved onto the Selenium story. In the end, it was clear-cut and all three engineers came to the conclusion that selenium was the better option.*

*I found having all of them swarming on each story together allowed them to come to a better conclusion, as they were able to collaborate, have their religious battles, and move on to take "ownership" of this solution. In the end, this took our approach of Cucumber driving the Selenium Webdriver to a new level towards what I felt was a legitimate enterprise-level automation framework.*

---

I realize that we spent quite a lot of real estate in this chapter talking about automation. That was intentional because it's simply that important within your Three Pillars strategy. In my view, you can't be agile if you aren't investing in it. Moving on from automation, I want to explore acceptance tests next as a significant extension to agile requirements.

## Acceptance Test-Driven Development

Let's not forget how simple, yet powerful, the notion of <u>conditions of acceptance</u> are when added to the construct of a user story. These are from a business or the customers' perspective. They help refine the feature into a set of criteria that adds and measures value. Often, they articulate "business logic" that is incredibly helpful for the developer(s) and tester(s) on a team to effectively design, code, test, and deliver the exact value proposition for each story.

---

[10] Here is the reference site for Watir – http://watir.com/ and here is the reference for Selenium Webdriver – http://docs.seleniumhq.org/docs/03_webdriver.jsp . Both are UI centric automation tools that take a UI based, top down approach in automating applications.

Another way of saying it is, interpreting the "just-in-time" and "just-enough" nature associated with each story. They help to focus the team on what is truly important and, if articulated properly, on making functional trade-off decisions. Independent of which *agile flavor one is implementing*[11], I've found the user story to be a wonderful approach to articulating requirements and the acceptance tests are a powerful part of the user story structure.

When you're deciding on your strategy for implementing Acceptance Test-Driven Development, please put your stories first. Learning to write them well, decompose them well, plan them well, and articulate acceptance criteria, or acceptance tests well is a crucial skill for your agile teams. And this skill needs to be learned before you invest heavily in ATDD or BDD automation. It's this *put your stories first* strategy that I've found most helpful in successful organizational transformations.

## Common ATDD Anti-Patterns

As the lead-in story in the books introduction highlighted, ATDD and its variant activities can be grossly misunderstood in agile contexts. Organizations have a tendency to make the following mistakes:

1. They consider it primarily a tooling and automation play and immediately dive into tools selection and writing as many automated tests as possible. Another variation of this anti-pattern is focusing totally on the ATDD tooling as the vehicle for writing ALL of their test automation.
2. They forget to include the "customer" or Product Owner in the development of acceptance criteria. This would include making them a part of training, tool selection, and writing the tests. Frequently, the technical teams themselves, in their fervor to implement ATDD, write all of the tests.
3. While the first two involved diving in too aggressively, I also see many teams that don't do anything regarding ATDD. They ignore the acceptance criteria part of their user story writing and then let this cascade throughout their usage. Another

---

[11] The User Story was initially defined in Extreme Programming. However, now the agile requirement artifact has nearly become the pervasive way to capture, discuss, and deliver agile functionality across ALL of the methods.

variation on this is hoping that unit and functional/feature level testing covers all aspects of story testing.

Let me share a story from Mary related to a sub-set of ATDD called Behavior-Driven Development, which was first coined by *Dan North*[12]. The most important part of this story is not the BDD specifics, but the benefits that Mary realized as a result of her experience.

## Mary's Corner

*At the heart of BDD is a rethinking of the approach to unit testing and acceptance testing that Dan North came up with while dealing with these issues.*

*For example, he proposed that unit test names be whole sentences starting with the word "should" and should be written in order of business value. Acceptance tests should be written using the standard agile framework of a user story: "As a [role], I want [feature], so that I realize some [benefit]". Acceptance criteria should be written in terms of scenarios and implemented as classes: Given [initial context], when [event occurs], then [ensure some outcomes].[1]*

*Starting from this point, North and others developed the BDD frameworks. Over a period of years, they framed it as a communication and collaboration framework for developers, testers, and other non-technical or business participants, to leverage in software projects.*

*The true value here is that the user story and acceptance tests are written as BDD format examples. These examples can be taken to backlog refinement meetings for the team to discuss, dissect, expand, understand, and eventually estimate.*

---

[12] Here's a link to in introduction to BDD techniques on Dan's website: http://dannorth.net/introducing-bdd/

*Having implemented BDD in now three different companies, I can say the benefits have been:*

- *Expectations, Goals and Business Value are communicated and challenged and clarified with every story (building the right thing the first time)*
- *Defined Scope*
- *Overlooked Requirements Revealed*
- *Tangible Reference Materials*
- *Accurate Story and Task Estimations*
- *Deliberate Collaboration Between QA/DEV/PO*
- *Increased Productivity*
- *Decreased Bugs from SIT/UAT/PROD*
- *Commitments are met (and often times exceeded!)*

## Setting Up a Separate "Automation Team"

I often get asked how do you attack test automation in a truly agile environment? For example, do you setup an automation centric Scrum team that is focused on automation infrastructure? Or, do you create a backlog of automation infrastructure stories and spread them across multiple teams?

The key decision here is whether automation work should be localized to a unique and often separate team.

Under normal circumstances, my answer is always no. I prefer the automation model to be similar to the model I've seen best applied to software architecture and UX within agile organizations. That is, you can have a small team that works on the architectural and overall design guidance, but then shares that in a crosscutting fashion across their teams. Often these folks move temporarily into the teams to instantiate their architecture and designs. Theirs is a part-time, forward-looking, and research role, but they need to engage and help the team's realize their vision.

I prefer exactly the same view for automation architecture, design, and infrastructural development. Yes, you might have a small team setting the direction, but the automation action and work should be mostly within your agile execution teams. Automation is best delivered by making it a part of everyone's job. This suggests a "balancing act" between the two focuses.

Another way of saying it is, "I don't like specialized automation teams who throw automation over the wall to your other agile teams". This is simply another example of a functional silo and subsequent hand-offs that agility is trying to break down and eliminate.

## *Attacking Automation Technical Debt*

The key thing is to get all types of technical debt, development and testing centric, on your product backlogs. That way you share with the business the true costs associated with their project and product work so they can make informed trade-off decisions.

Another huge part of this is providing explanation and justification, in clear business and customer value terms, as to what the impact of the work will be. For example, "Trust me, this automation needs more refactoring..." is not a solid enough case for technical debt work. You have to be empathetic and put on the voice of the customer in cost-justifying your work.

I realize that's hard sometimes, but it's important to make as honest an effort as you can in connecting your debt work to your business stakeholders.

---

### Mary's Corner

*Bob, I feel like you downplayed this section way too much. Every time I walk into a QA organization, I walk into huge automation technical debt. I once walked into an organization that had six automation toolsets on ten different scrum teams. We ended up creating over 300 user stories to tackle the debt they had built up.*

*These user stories stemmed from converting all their old automated tests to the new tool that was selected, for missing automated regression, for high severity defects missed over the past years releases, and for re-writing old unit and integration tests in the new framework. It was a ton of work. We prioritized it; we created a roadmap with goals and a timeframe, and then started to execute it.*

*One key thing to mention for those in senior leadership positions – this test debt just like code debt had built up over time; therefore, it will take time to fix it all. There is no magic bullet. There are releases where there will be no QA debt recovery due to market demand, but maybe after a few bribed Product Owners you will get there.*

*No really, bribery goes a long way! Ok, what I really mean here is that partnering with the Product Owners, and getting their buy-in, and figuring how to get your debt prioritized on the team backlog just like the other forms of debt. This has been historically one of the hardest parts of my job. It is not an easy task. It takes education, time, and PO's willing to learn about agile QA practices.*

*Showing them and the engineering managers that the benefit of paying down QA technical debt is just as important as development debt and customer features. If you're successful, this investment in the long term pays off by reduced post release issues, higher velocity, and most importantly, more satisfied customers.*

## Information Radiators

The notion of an information radiator is unique to agile methods. The first references to them came from Alistair Cockburn in his *Crystal*[13] work. It's a simple concept really—if there are details that teams, leadership, and the organization "care about", then it might make sense to radiate them so everyone can see the resulting data.

Often this takes the shape of physical charts and pictures on the walls of your office space. The quintessential Scrum Board with its swim lanes, stories and tasks, impediment list and burndown chart(s), is a wonderful example of an information radiator. *Figure 6* is an example of a "physical board" to help you visualize the concept.

---

[13] Crystal, and it's Clear and colored variations, is an agile methodology that Alistair created. It's not been very popular in the community, but it has some practices and thinking models that are quite useful. This is one of them.

Source: http://mhjongerius.tumblr.com/post/16222404998/our-new-product-backlog-wall
Figure 6, Example of Organizational Scrum of Scrums "Wall Radiator"

In this example, there are team specific areas, release specific areas, information from their Scrum of Scrums, and their overall Enterprise-level product backlog. There intent here is to "radiate" all relevant software deliver information from one linear wall. Very cool if you ask me!

I'll leave it as an exercise for you to develop effective radiators that meet the needs of your various constituents. I would recommend a multi-tiered strategy (imagine that) here, as well. One where you show:

- Detailed testing coverage at all levels of the pyramid; it should also be aggregated.
- Detailed manual testing, exploratory testing, and other non-functional testing progress.
- Backlogs related to your technical debt and technical test debt—including progress vs. plan indicators.
- Backlogs related to your infrastructure strategy and development plans. Put up a quarterly release plan and show progress against your milestones.

- Furthermore, always connect the dots between your product releases and your automation efforts. Showing how those efforts are improving quality, workflow, predictable releases, and value delivery.

One of my favorite information radiators is illustrated in an article written by Jeff Patton where he showed "smiley faces" to reflect how the testers felt about the components of an application they were testing. Smiles were a reflection of high confidence and frowns were a reflection of defects and lower confidence.

The team kept these indicators up-to-date, in real-time, as they continued to test each of the components. The information radiator in this case was simple...but extremely effective. Their developer colleagues took it as a personal challenge to turn the frowns upside down. Anyone who walked by the radiator clearly understood the stability of each area of the application. I have a link to the article in the reference section, as it remains one of my favorite examples of a creative, simple, and effective information radiator.

Another key is having real-time displays of your CI/CD systems and automation results all over your team rooms and areas. It might cost a bit to gain this level of transparency, but the impact the information radiators have on your organization, are typically...priceless.

## Mary's Corner

*I was new to the same firm that Bob discussed in the introduction, and was assigned to a project that was "all in" with automation, continuous integration, and information radiators. We had over 1000 tests, which were growing everyday. I was happy to be walking into a project that was so dedicated to automation and transparency. It was exciting! But, on the first day, I asked why all the builds where red on the displays?*

*One of the testers mentioned that someone checked in bad code that broke a few tests. I said "Great! We must be automating the right things". I assume the developer is <u>stopping the line</u> and fixing their code to make the tests green? The tester said they weren't sure when he was going to fix it. At that point, I went directly to the development manager and asked* *why they weren't fixing the bad code that was checked in because they broke our tests. The manager said—*

*"Why, the tests have never been green? Most of the time they are broken because of bad, or poorly written, tests or environment issues; almost never because of our code." I said, "Can you prove it?" He then said, " No, but 99% of time QA is just crying wolf".*

*At this point, our information radiators had zero value. The radiators were always red, no one actively worked on the failures, and all the automation might as well have never been created because nobody really cared.*

*I spent the next six months working on a culture change. I evangelized the value of the radiators, negotiated user stories to fix the fragile tests, and also negotiated user stories to fix the wrongly configured environments. I asked the QA team to train the developers on the automation framework so that they could help fix tests and understand the safety net the tests gave them. I influenced stop-the-line behavior when a build was broken.*

*When over 1200 tests went green, and information radiators for 16 builds were all green, I bought the entire development and QA teams pizza. I also bought them pizza the following week it went green again - because that's how long it took for it to happen. After that, the teams and managers bought into the value of automation and QA "never cried wolf" again.*

---

Mary's story connects well to the other pillars and to an overall mindset within your teams. One key to information radiators is the transparency it creates and the subsequent conversations it inspires. I literally can't describe how powerful this can be in operation. So if you're looking for an "effectiveness metric" for you information radiators, it's:

> *Is the organization <u>paying attention</u> to them, are they creating <u>conversations</u>, and are they <u>driving action</u>?*

## References

- A nice review of the history behind the Pyramid – http://blog.goneopen.com/2010/08/test-automation-pyramid-review/
- Wonderful discussion of the Automation Ice Cream Cone Anti-pattern – http://watirmelon.com/2012/01/31/introducing-the-software-testing-ice-cream-cone/
- A short, but pithy recent weigh-in by Martin Fowler – http://martinfowler.com/bliki/TestPyramid.html
- Mike Cohn revisits it – http://www.mountaingoatsoftware.com/blog/the-forgotten-layer-of-the-test-automation-pyramid
- The link to the Jeff Patton "Smiley" article I mentioned earlier – http://www.stickyminds.com/article/simple-strategies-keep-quality-visible
- And a wonderful blog post by Gojko Adzic about Visualizing Quality - http://gojko.net/2011/04/27/visualising-quality-initial-ideas/

# Chapter 3 – Pillar #2:

# Software Testing

Pillar 2 is focused towards the craft, the profession, and the art of software testing. I often see an organization's view of testing decline when they decide to adopt agile methods. While not totally understanding the drivers for that trend, I see it over and over again.

One guess of the root cause lies within the early genesis of the methods being driven mostly by developers. Clearly, early agile efforts minimized software testing under the assumption that it would be "rolled into" the developers work activity. To be honest, there's still a fair bit of that viewpoint around today. That narrow view has been exacerbated by such organizations as Microsoft, Google, and Facebook who are famously not hiring testers, but instead, hiring Software Developers in Test (SDET's).

Another challenge has been the narrowing of what testing means in an agile environment. It also relates to the above. Many agile teams consider agile testing to only include:

- Unit-level testing; including perhaps automating the unit tests;
- Functional level testing at a User Story level;
- Story Acceptance-level testing; and
- On-the-fly Continuous Integration leveraging common CI tooling.

Testing often stops after these steps are accomplished within each team and sprint. Now, in certain contexts, for example, small web based products that are relatively new, this may well be all that is needed. But in many, many more contexts, there is a lot more testing activity that is required. Repetitive testing of previously delivered functionality is also a consideration that is often lost in the frenzy of delivering "done" software within each sprint.

What I'm trying to focus on in Pillar Two is the fact that there is so much more to professional software testing than is typically thought of in agile teams. In addition, I'd want to convince you not to discard your traditional testing strategies when you move to agile. Yes, testing in an agile environment is certainly different and yes, it requires adjustments of just about all of your testing tactics, tools, and strategies.

But, throwing those hard-won skills away or ignoring them is not a prudent or responsible option.

The other critical piece, and it's a pervasive point across all three pillars, is that you don't test-in quality! Instead you build it in. Beyond testing tactics, we need to emphasize quality based tactics and thinking, as well.

For example, reviews are a proven activity that yields great results in quality improvement. This would include constructing and exposing designs and prototypes for review. So, yes, there would be a basis of "working code", as per the Agile Manifesto, but also a focus on team-wide work transparency and collaborative reviews.

*Figure 7* provides an overview of the focus for this pillar.

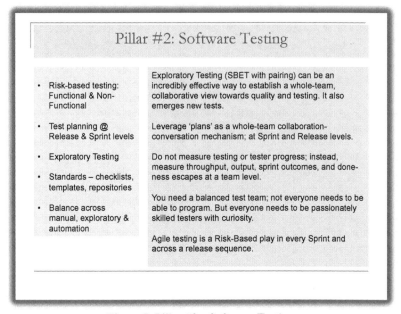

Figure 7, Pillar #2 – Software Testing

Now, at this point, I want to start diving into more of the specific practices or tactics that reside within this pillar.

## Risk-Based Testing

Before all of the agile hoopla, I worked for a company that was delivering a data analysis application for various types of news feeds for specific customer niches. One was publishing, then pharmaceutical, and finally, the legal domain. I joined the firm as the Director of QA, although the title was inflated as I had a fairly small team, at least when compared with the number of developers. Here's a story surrounding risk-based testing in that environment:

*Within my first week, the team and I were asked to plan for testing an upcoming release. When I reviewed:*

- *The skills we had for testing (and those we didn't);*
- *The amount of functionality the development team was delivering;*
- *What we "knew" about the scope and complexity of the new functionality;*
- *And, the amount of testing my small team could accomplish in the allotted time. (There was a firm release date...imagine that!)*

*I quickly realized that we could only test about 45% of the "stuff" that we would have liked to test under more normal conditions. Most of the gap surrounded not having the skills and time.*

*Initially, the test team was incredibly stressed out about the gap. They began talking about working overtime and missing their families in order to get more done. I stopped most of that thinking and simply wanted to plan our testing with a slightly over normal workload. I just didn't feel it fair to severely impact the test team's personal lives by a maniacal drive for "100% coverage", which we couldn't meet anyway.*

*What we did next is put together a "Risk Based" testing plan. We basically made a list of all of the things we thought needed to be tested. That included functional, and non-functional requirements like performance and security. Then, we prioritized the work and drew a "cut line" based on our teams' realistic capacity.*

*One of the things that didn't get prioritized was performance testing, primarily because we didn't have the tooling, or the expertise, within the team to do it. As with any good risk-based testing or RBT approach, we scheduled a meeting with all of our project stakeholders and reviewed what we planned on testing. I remember the reactions as if it were yesterday.*

*The feedback from the cross-functional team and stakeholders was that everything on our list was important and it **ALL** needed to be tested. (Of course that's what they wanted.) I politely pointed out that that wasn't an* *option. Given a fixed time and a fixed team project, we had to modify testing coverage scope in order to support the date.*

*It wasn't that we didn't want to test everything; it was that it just wasn't possible. So given that reality we, as a leadership team, needed to make some hard decisions; decisions that inevitably involved taking on some risk.*

*The other options for our decision(s) included:*

- *Change the delivery date.*
- *Reduce the number of delivered features.*
- *Get the developers to "pitch in" and help with the testing.*

*All of which were soundly laughed at and dismissed. No problem I said; then we can only test 45% of our plan. Furthermore, we can't do any performance testing because we lack the expertise. So, let's "roll up our sleeves" and figure out how to maximize the impact of that 45%!*

---

Eventually we worked through it, but it turned out that this was the first time someone in the testing team had ever challenged the project level team to make a trade-off call. I was determined, but astounded at the same time.

You see life in testing is all about risk-based testing. You never have all of the time or people to test everything. It's always a question of what, when, and how much. I look back on this incident and fondly recall an organization that grew up very quickly—starting to make much more mature decisions from a testing investment perspective.

## *Fast Forward to Agile Testing*

Fast-forward to when I first encountered agile and the implication that it had to the discipline of testing; it quickly struck me as a wonderful, risk-based testing play. At its core, you're testing bits of an application as they're developed. Each sprint you have three competing "prime directives":

1. How do we effectively test the features being delivered in this sprint?

2. How do we effectively regression test the features that have already been delivered and tested?

3. How do we effectively do integration testing across teams that are operating in our product ecosystem?

Clearly number one is the most straightforward of these directives, while two and three are moving targets. The easiest answer for them would be to perform a full regression and full integration tests each and every sprint. However, that would be incredibly expensive and often, due to the size of the testing effort, virtually impossible to fit into a single sprint.

By definition, agile testing is all about risk-based testing. It's about prioritization, communication, and collaboration surrounding the right set of tests to run within each sprint. The primary way to handle that surrounds the product backlog. If you've read my Scrum Product Ownership book, you know that I recommend a model where all work, (and I mean <u>all work</u>) that a team is doing for a software project should surface on the backlog.

As they refine their backlogs for each sprint and release, each team discusses testing at a story level, sprint level, and release level. While planning testing work, the risk-based testing efforts are captured as notes and activities within the estimates for each story. The team adjusts its capacity, in other words how much they take on each sprint, by the amount of testing each requires.

You see the <u>team decides</u> on the risk proposition. They do this based upon:

- Their adherence to their Definition-of-Done;
- Their understanding of the application and the requisite quality needed to meet the customers' needs;
- Their professional judgment;
- Cross-team dependencies, if any;
- And finally, the business case for it; which is usually represented by the Product Owners' understanding of the customer, i.e., the Just-Enough Quality view.

They make their decisions visible to their Product Owner, as well as, their business stakeholders. Then, sprint-by-sprint, they deliver on those goals.

If you have a legacy of techniques or practices that are focused towards risk-based testing, please don't throw them away or stop leveraging them when you "go Agile". I hope to have convinced you that RBT is alive and well within agile contexts. In fact, it's the requisite approach to the testing.

## Mary's Corner

*Bob, I don't think QA testers fundamentally understand risk-based testing concepts. Most testers will say they do risk-based testing because they were simply not able to get to everything they wanted to test in a sprint therefore they release the software anyway.*

*To me, risk-based testing means defining what you're NOT going to test and prioritizing the most technically complex and highest customer value features first. At the end of the day, I want my testers to be able to tell me what areas of the application are at risk by making objective decisions on what not to test instead of "guessing" that they did not need to test that area in the first place.*

*The other important aspect in effective risk-based testing is gaining cross-team accountability as to what needs to be tested and how much versus what isn't. In other words – balancing the risk. And by cross-team I mean the developers, product owners, customers, stakeholders, etc.*

*One of the measures of effective risk-based testing is that nobody <u>blames</u> QA for not testing the right things or for not finding a bug; it's a cross-team responsibility.*

Now, let's move onto a very practical and useful testing technique that can become a valuable part of your arsenal when performing your agile risk-based testing.

## *Exploratory Testing*

In 2009, when I took over as Director of Software Development at iContact, I inherited a team that had been using Scrum for a couple of years. Unfortunately, it was a "development only" effort and the testers were testing outside of the Scrum teams. One of the first actions I took was integrating the two groups into truly cross-functional Scrum teams. In conjunction with that, I introduced the notion of Exploratory Testing (or ET) as a testing technique.

In our case, we performed ET in pairs and, normally, that included a tester and a developer. Beyond the testing, the pairing helped establish a whole-team view towards testing that was instrumental in our agile evolution. Exploratory Testing, from my perspective, is a technique that has great value beyond simply "testing". It reinforces cross-team collaboration, pairing, quality, and a healthy respect for, and learning of, the craft of testing. In the end, everyone is focused towards <u>how</u> the customer will be using the product and the <u>value</u> it delivers.

A fundamental requirement for Exploratory Testing is domain experience. For example, if you brought in a team of college interns to test your stock trading system application and they have no trading experience, than ET is not the testing approach you should be using. They would have no clue surrounding your domain and, therefore, their explorations in this case would be near valueless. In fact, they might have a negative effect by draining your core team in answering their questions.

If on the other hand, you have a strong testing team with years of domain experience, then this technique might be incredibly valuable to you. Don't misunderstand me, not everyone on the team has to have strong domain experience. In fact, ET will help in cross-training your testers while helping your teams increase their overall understanding of the business domain.

But I'm getting a bit ahead of myself. Let's define and explore the history of ET a bit more.

## A Little History and Definition

Manual, ad-hoc testing has been practiced for as long as there has been software to test. Exploratory Testing is not ad-hoc testing. Ad-hoc testing creates no written results either before or after the testing. You simply "bang on" an application randomly until you find a bug. Quite often the testers cannot clearly articulate how they found the bug, which frustrates the efforts to reproduce and repair it.

ET on the other hand, keeps a log or detailed notes of the testers travels. Sometimes written notes, but often screen shots, UI interaction logs, and snippets of system log files augment the information that is captured during the testing. So, no scripts or test cases are driving the testing, but full details of what was tested are constructed along the way.

*James Bach* [14]is considered the father of Exploratory Testing while his brother Jon Bach, is considered the father of the sessions extension or Session-Based Exploratory Testing (SBET). When I say Exploratory Testing, I'm really referring to SBET and will continue that going forward.

## SBET in a Nutshell

Here are the essential steps for performing Session-Based Exploratory Testing; sort of an "in a nutshell" version:

1. First, you decompose your *Application Under Test* to fairly discrete areas that encompass all of the functional areas for your Application.
2. You identify these areas with a name or *Charter*[15]. You might add a few sentences describing what testing is "in play" and not "in play" with respect to testing this specific charter.

---

[14] You can find out more about James and Exploratory Testing by visiting his website: www.satisfice.com

[15] Sometimes Session-Based Exploratory Testing is called Charter-Based Exploratory Testing. The charters are the "units" of focus or work that is planned, executed, and reported out on.

3. A good rule of thumb is to associate a charter with an area you can test within a session, thus the session-based addition. Common session time-boxes are 60-90-120 minutes.
4. The list of charters should completely cover ALL functional aspects of your application.
5. Often a risk-based approach is taken when prioritizing or ordering charters. Usually, it's based on what has recently been introduced in the latest increment of your product.
6. In order to test, you then have a team, individually or in pairs, pick up a charter and test it for your session time-box intervals.
7. During the sessions, the testers log their discoveries.
8. After a group executes their charters, there is an SBET, session de-brief where results are discussed across all of the testers. Often, if you're planning on multiple sessions running, the results of one session will influence adjustments in subsequent sessions.
9. Finally, all bugs found during the SBET should be reported and acted upon.

One final point, SBET should only be a part of your overall testing strategy. As I'll get into in the next section, having a broad testing focus including manual and automated techniques is probably your best strategy.

## Mary's Corner

*I had heard about exploratory sessions and SBET sessions, but never had seen them done in practice until I arrived at iContact. They had SBET sessions, which they called "Test Fests", scheduled the first day of hardening sprints with all of the Scrum team's participating. The QA team would hand out the charters and goals, primarily playing the role of SBET strategist, while the developers would be the primary ones to explore.*

*This was wonderful to be a part of! It encouraged the whole team approach to quality, and the developers were able to find many defects quickly so they could fix them the remainder of the hardening sprint.*

*Since leaving, I've used these planned "Test Fests" in many ways. I use them for multi-team Scrum projects when all the integration points have first been implemented. I often use them right before we release these projects to Beta customers. Sometimes, I even plan one in the middle of a Scrum sprint just to get a feeling about whether or not we are integrating early and often. I think the key here is knowing when and why to call a "Test Fest" and who should be included.*

*A good rule of thumb is to call for one when more than two scrum teams are involved, and you are about to release the code to a pre-production area. It's amazing how many bugs you find when people start to focus on pair testing.*

## Test Strategy, Plans, and Cases – Oh My!

One of the most overlooked practices in agile testing is "test planning". Yes, I said it...Planning!

In my experience, very few teams actually do any test planning within their agile iterations or releases. Instead they mostly focus on story-at-a-time testing. Rarely is a holistic view taken as to how they'll approach testing strategy leading towards meeting their overall release goals.

Consider it the same as code architectural or design phases, applied to the testing effort. Also, if they do plan, it's usually the testers doing it in a vacuum rather than the whole-team thoughtfully considering the testing implications for their sprint-by-sprint commitments.

At iContact, our testing team took that approach. For each sprint, the testers would pull together a wiki-based test plan that covered the body of work the team had committed to. I remember there was one team that failed a few sprints because of underestimating the testing required to meet our overall Definition-of-Done. When I spoke to the team about it, they were essentially unapologetic—implying that they had done everything possible to mitigate testing. When asked about the plan, everyone said, yes, they'd done one. When the developers were asked what part they had played, they coyly said they had briefly reviewed it, and signed off on the "tester's plan".

I stopped things at that moment and explained that we wanted each team to do a test strategy or plan as part of their overall commitment to each sprint. That it needed to be written down and discussed as a team. The important point was neither the words nor the page count. Instead, the most important point was for the <u>whole-team</u> to collaborate around <u>their strategies</u> for delivering a sound, well crafted, and high quality body of work that met their sprint commitments. It shouldn't be the testers test plan; it should be the team's test plan.

Essentially, every agile team should do this. Sure, we prefer that they write it down and keep it, but the words are secondary to the discussion, collaboration, and actively moving these strategies into the teams work plans for each sprint.

But, then again, Mary has a counterpoint story to tell...

## Mary's Corner

*Bob implemented this test strategy approach before I got to iContact but, by the time I got fully engrained into the process, all teams were still not doing it. Most teams were waiting until hardening, or the exploratory testing phase, to collaborate on what testing had been done and what was left. Also, the test plans had become more of our regression tests and were used as charters for exploratory testing, which as we all know is sort of wrong.*

*Bob says I broke his heart when I stopped this test planning technique to do more of a risk based testing strategy approach. I believed we were having overkill of documentation that no one ever read or maintained after the initial conversation. Agile says be lean on the documentation and only create documentation that you will maintain. Bob's goal in the end was to create a sprint and release level conversation with the whole team about all testing activities that had to be completed.*

*In my opinion, this should be covered in well-written user stories (including user stories that might say: "As a tester I want to perform system integration testing to ensure that all functions still work.") for each sprint or hardening sprint. I believe that all non-functional requirements should be included in the user story and as acceptance criteria. I also believe that your regression tests get built up every sprint because the Definition-of-Done should include that they are automated.*

*But, let's get this straight. I am NOT saying you do not need to create test plans. What I am saying, is to have testing conversations in backlog refinement, have well written user stories, and include in the acceptance criteria all the testing that you are planning to do. Have conversations in planning about what testing is happening, as well as, when and what QA might need from development, so they can finish the story the fastest. To Bob's point have a conversation on the test plan or strategy with the whole-team at some point before you commit and start a sprint.*

*You might ask – So, what did I do? Did I stop? I say I just did something comparable; Bob says I stopped.*

*On Day 1 of a sprint, I had the testers essentially create a feature, or story based outline, of all the tests they wanted to conduct. Then I had them review the list with QA members on the other Scrum teams to make sure there was no overlap of repetitive testing.*

*I also had them review the items with the developers and Product Owner(s) on their Scrum team. Bob would say this was risky, as after all of the reviews, testing might have committed to more than we could actually do. That's where the risked-based testing would come in. We would negotiate the testing that was mandatory and take risks. We did not test items that weren't critical. If it was decided that all items were mandatory, then we would re-plan the sprint, but this almost never happened as developers would help, or we could get help from other team members on others teams, that were not full up in their current sprint.*

*In the end, we had only two severity one issues for the whole next year; both happened to be legacy issues that got exposed implementing new code. So, in my opinion, it worked. I have, and will continue to implement, this technique in the future; I feel it is a practical agile testing technique that reduces the paperwork traditional test planning introduces and will be read more than one time after it is created.*

*You will say this won't work in a regulatory environment. It might not work in all, but I beg to differ it won't work in most. I worked for a year and a half at a bank in which I wrote a test strategy document for the product in general. Then, I wrote test outlines, test cases for each sprint to say what was tested, and then I provided results. That was enough for the auditors.*

---

While it may not read that way, Mary and I do share the same perspective. Agile teams need to apply whole-team planning (and ownership) to development, as well as, testing activity. Whether it's written down or not isn't the point. It's the act of collaborative planning and discussion that is important. I think of the Dwight Eisenhower quote here as the point, paraphrasing as:

*Plans are worth <u>nothing</u>, but Planning is worth <u>everything</u>*

## *Release Planning*

In agile at-scale, there are planning events usually held that pull the entire group of teams together to plan a focused release. In SAFe, the event is a called *Release Train Planning,* or *PSI Planning* (Potentially Shippable Increment). If you were operating in an Extreme Programming shop years ago, it would simply have been called Release Planning. That's what I call it today when I implement it in Scrum environments that are leveraging Scrum of Scrums for scaling.

Whatever you call it, the activity is focused on taking a look across multiple sprints, and if you have multiple teams, across those teams. The common denominator in release planning is that the teams are working on a product or project leveraging shared and integrated codebases. When that's the case, the release planning not only examines each teams' individual efforts, but the cross-team efforts to produce a shippable product.

Therefore, release planning is often focused towards:

- Dependencies;
- Integration testing;
- Regression, System, and Non-functional testing;
- Cross team Architecture, UX, and DevOps activity;
- System level Demo orchestration;

- Organizational planning and readiness activity leading to a full (production-level) release.

While testing planning is important at a sprint-level, from my perspective, it's simply crucial in at-scale, multiple team scenarios. In these cases, there are considerations beyond simply delivering working code at the end of each sprint. More traditional testing phases often come into play and need to be articulated, captured in the release plan, and in your working product backlogs.

A test strategy or approach needs to cover integration and non-functional requirements. Strategies for testing early need to surface, but not necessarily continuously. For example, in performance testing, you'll want the team to sort out the right strategy for testing performance throughout the release train.

What's the earliest possible moment? What's the latest responsible moment that includes time for adjustments? Are there opportunities for efficiently testing for performance as part of each sprint? These are things that we want the team to be thoughtful about.

Then, the overriding viewpoint is "production" – so release planning shouldn't be solely focused on making it work in "development". It must also be thoughtful about the operating environments; therefore, a DevOps perspective needs to be included in the teams' strategies.

## *Concept of a "Release Train"*

From a testing perspective, one of the most useful constructs that has come out of the scaled agile space are two notions:

1. The notion of a **Release Train**. This is a planning framework where you connect a series of sprints together to move from a truly iterative development to a production-ready release. The term was coined by Dean Leffingwell in his Scaling Software Agility (2007) book and has carried forward to his Scaled Agile Framework. Typically in SAFe, a release train might be composed of 4-5, 2-week development focused sprints. Then, right before release, there would be a 2-week sprint focused on hardening (as explained next).

2. The notion of **Hardening Sprints**. For years, there have been debates in the agile community as to the "agility" of leveraging Hardening (or Stabilization) Sprints in your release trains or release tempo. SAFe includes them, in v2.5 as something called a "HIP" (Hardening-Innovation-Planning) sprint. In v3.0 of SAFe, they are "blending" the hardening across the development sprints and have changed the name to an "IP" sprint. In either case, the sprints provide a pause for running, what I would call classic, broader scale testing such as full integration, regression, and system tests. Which in some contexts, for example: financial, medical, or insurance domains, this testing is mandated by government regulations.

I find that the testers, in agile contexts, can make a huge difference by contributing to the activities associated with expanding each release train and its associated hardening sprints.

In my opinion, this is where traditional testing strategy <u>lives</u> and I expect the testers to develop, socialize, and to integrate with the release train milestones and goals. But, beyond that, to make it a whole-team exercise where everyone has agreed on a sufficient amount of testing and stabilization required pre-release.

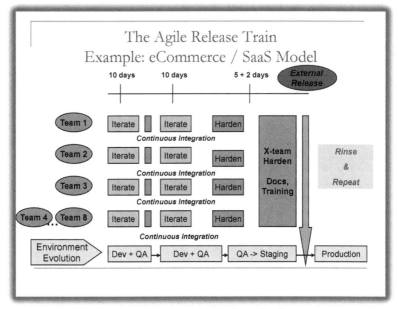

Figure 8, Example of Release Train

*Figure 8* is an example of a release train tempo. In this case, it's relatively short, about 25 days, or a little over a month. Approximately every 30 days this organization is pushing out a production-level release. The train is composed of two, 2-week development sprints, followed by a 1-week hardening sprint. There are some pre-production steps that take another 2 days and after that, their application is pushed.

You can see the environment promotion steps along the base of the diagram. This is how the code is maturing from a testing environment perspective. You should also note that Continuous Integration is also active. This is simply an example of a release train. Pre-release, all eight of the teams would get together to plan their individual and cross-team responsibilities focused on creating a thoughtful, well integrated, well tested, and cohesive release.

## *Test Artifacts in General*

If you extrapolate the planning guidance Mary and I have provided, I think it also seeps into test case design, test documentation, automation design and documentation; literally every other testing-centric artifact your might create. A common agile myth is to drop all of your testing documentation and I've seen that anti-pattern incredibly often. The key point is to <u>lean</u> your documentation and move the decision-making into the team as to what, and how much, to document. But, <u>that</u> you document, is more of an organizational decision. Please make this point in your Definition-of-Done.

Another key point is that any test-centric documentation needs to pass muster across the team; no longer do testers solely determine them. For example, the developers need to understand the need for, and how to write, test cases and then check them into the testing repository—if that is part of the organizations context for handling tests. This would extend to test design and any other artifacts that the testers feel are required.

One final point in this section and it overrides all documentation that you'll produce. The value is not in the documentation. Nor, do you want your testers filling in templates in lieu of thinking and collaborating. The point of documentation is to drive thinking, planning, risk consideration, engagement with your customer, and ultimately, how to deliver on your promises. Documents are a means to an end, and in an agile context, that end is working, high-value, high quality code.

Therefore, the documentation you produce is <u>for</u> the team and <u>not for</u> management or the process. Encourage your team to document when and where necessary and then trust their professionalism and craftsmanship in making solid documentation decision-making.

## Mary's Corner

*We don't really call out test cases or test case management here. I am still surprised with how many QA engineers stop creating test cases when they adopt agile approaches. I always ask the question, "Where is the living documentation and how does the system work?" to the QA engineers; they usually respond with the release notes.*

*I am not sure about you, but the release notes rarely go over negative testing scenarios and/or what happens when customers use the software the wrong way. I often walk into organizations using Google spreadsheets and Wiki pages of test cases and a test case management tool that nobody uses.*

*Since I am a proponent for BDD tools like Cucumber and Specflow, I no longer buy test case management tools. Instead, I store my test cases along side the developers code and tests in the same source control system. That way, you have living documentation with the code itself.*

*With that said, there is never an excuse to not write test cases! If, not for the sole reason, when your tester with the most years tenure decides to walk out the door, you know where to look to see how the system is supposed to work.*

---

I can't believe I'm doing this, but I absolutely agree, and disagree, with Mary. I want both of these to occur – agile documentation on its own <u>and</u> code aligned documentation. In other words, do what makes sense in your context, but be responsible. I'm not sure where the propensity to avoid documentation has come from in our agile adoption efforts, but documentation is OK in my book. It's not a bad thing as long as we are lean and responsible.

## *Moving to 'Agile' Metrics*

If you look back on my basic definition of this pillar, you noticed that test metrics were there. I simply can't leave the chapter without, at least, touching on them. However, I do want to share something that I often struggle with. As teams "go Agile", there are some activities and practices that need to fundamentally change as a result. In my view, one of these is the metrics your organization collects and values.

In pre-agile organizations it is often the case that <u>individual functions</u> are measured. For example:

- **Architects** might be measured by their designs, meetings, documents produced, phase-gates supported, or attainment of specific milestones;
- **Business Analysts** might be measured by requirements, use cases, or logic guides written; wireframes designed, or attainment of specific milestones;
- **Developers** might be measured by lines of code, components, bugs produced, or attainment of specific coding milestones;
- **Testers** might be measured by: test cases written, executed, bugs found, automation running, and attainment of specific testing milestones;
- **Documentation Writers** might be measured by: pages reviewed, pages written, and attainment of specific documentation milestones.

You get the idea. Each functional silo is uniquely measured. Often the Project Managers are measured as a means of "gluing" all of these silos together towards a project level release goal. However, the measures are often not unified or aligned, and they certainly don't measure delivery from a concept-to-cash or throughput perspective, which is ultimately how our customers are measuring us.

Post-agile measurement is different. Instead of measuring functional silo's and work as it completes each phase, we want to measure it more holistically. Post-agile measurements should try to focus on four fundamental areas:

1. **Predictability** – How is the <u>team</u> performing at a delivery or throughput level? Are they predictably delivering on their Release Planned commitments? Can they accurately articulate and anticipate their true capacity?

2. **Value Delivered** – Is the <u>team</u> getting the higher priority items first? Are stakeholders getting the chance to provide early feedback and see dynamic adjustments? Does the <u>team</u> embrace change to the customers' competitive advantage?

3. **Quality** – How is the <u>team</u> meeting their Definition-of-Done, quality, and overriding organizational goals? For example, are customer defect escapes declining? Are overall open defects declining? Customer surveys on satisfaction levels also play well here.

4. **Team Health** – Is the <u>team</u> motivated, energized, innovative, and excited about their customers and solutions? Is attrition low? Are job offer accept rates high? Is the organization clearly recognized as a "good place" to work? Employee surveys on satisfaction levels are crucial here.

These directly target the agile principles and are intentionally simple. Usually, an organization will define 1-2 key performance metrics in each of these areas, and then monitor them over time for validity. Metrics are intended to drive behavior, so the focus is on "paying attention to principles" and "continuous improvement", rather than on simply reporting and by-rote analysis paralysis. Agile metrics should also <u>drive action</u>.

In this case, notice that they are not specifically testing or tester metrics. They are whole-team metrics. Your testers should be measured by how they operate within their agile teams – driving software value that meets your Definition-of-Done and all of your quality goals. As a test leader who is chartered with moving their team and organization towards agile approaches, you'll want to de-emphasize traditional test metrics while emphasizing whole-team metrics along the lines of the four areas listed above.

One final point, does this shift matter? You bet it does. Team performance is strongly influenced by what and how you measure. If you measure each functional silo, you sub-optimize on the function. Solid agile metrics optimize on the whole. Partner across your functional organization to move from functionally based measures to team and delivery-based metrics. It will strongly influence your self-directed agile teams and ultimately your results.

---

## Mary's Corner

*In a previous company, I had a boss who loved metrics. Actually, the entire firm loved metrics. However, I never thought in a million years that I would have more conversations about metrics than I would about my teams' delivery success.*

*My first week on the job my boss said to me, "Mary what does 'good' look like for QA?" I was so excited that he had asked my opinion! Bob had just come up with the Three Pillars concept, post iContact, so I laid out the pillars to him. He said, " Great! Those are exactly my thoughts, as well." I walked out of that meeting thinking, that was way too easy – what's the catch?*

*A month went by and in my next one-on-one meeting with him, he asked me to show him my metrics. I asked him what he meant. I showed him the Three Pillars, along with all the things I was working on, to make us a high performing QA organization. He thought that was all well and good, but he needed the numbers to prove that I was doing what I said I'd be doing. I was perplexed. He then asked, "Where is your number of tests cases that were created, run, passed, failed for this last release? How many bugs did you find? How many bugs where still open? How much did you automate? How much do you have left to automate?" The questions just kept coming.*

*My response was that I had just gotten CI up and running. My QA teams are now starting to write test cases, and we just finalized our definition-of-done. He was shaking his head; I knew this was not going to be good, or easy, from this time on. Over the next year, I gave him four different sets of metrics – including the Forrester Agile Testing Assessment Tool. I thought an industry standard would make him happy and, for a while, it did. That was until I told him I had the team fill it out and not me. At that point he discredited it.*

*After some time went by, I received an email from him telling me that I was going to be a part of our Technology Centers' Metrics team. Basically, the company was selecting a few people for each technology center to come up with metrics to measure the each center against one other and to measure our software producing teams productivity and efficiency.*

*I was super excited! I would be paired up with some of the smartest people at the bank and would finally be able to give my boss the metrics he expected. I mean, he couldn't dispute the metrics we came up for the whole company right? Well, over the next two months, we had several meetings on agile metrics and created a white paper. In my opinion, we came up with about half of what Bob recommends and half things I would have never thought of. I left the bank before the metrics recommendation was finally reviewed and displayed, but in the end, I was told the metrics we came up with never went anywhere. Why you might ask, because what 'good' looks like differs for almost anyone that you ask.*

*So what's the moral of this story? Take Bob's recommendations for areas of metrics to concentrate on, get with the senior leadership in your organization, and ask them individually what 'good' looks like, and then define your metrics around that. Don't spend countless hours measuring things people don't care about.*

## *References*

- Any of the classic software testing books can provide insights into Risk-Based Testing (RBT) approaches and techniques. I'd recommend any by Cem Kaner or Rex Black. For example: Managing the Testing Process, by Rex Black, 3'rd Edition.

- Believe it or not, the Bach's really haven't written a definitive text surrounding Exploratory Testing. The best book about the technique right now is by Elisabeth Hendrickson, entitled: Explore It!

- Here's a link to James Bach's website which does contain guidance for Exploratory Testing and SBET – www.satisfice.com

- Here's a link to the Scaled Agile Framework – www.scaledagility.com

- Here's a link to the Forrester Agile Testing Assessment Tool that Mary references in one of her Corner's – http://www.forrester.com/Forresters+Agile+Testing+Maturity+Assessment+Tool/fulltext/-/E-RES90341

- I've written some explorations of Release Planning and Hardening Sprints that would augment that section. You can find them here:
  - Release Planning – http://rgalen.com/s/Types-of-Agile-End-to-End-Planning-v44h.pdf
  - Hardening Sprints – http://rgalen.com/s/AgileRecord_17_Galen.pdf

- Finally, here's a collection of blog posts that I've written or found useful surrounding agile metrics:
  - http://rgalen.com/agile-training-news/2014/4/22/2-dozen-weird-agile-metrics-ideas
  - http://rgalen.com/agile-training-news/2012/6/2/the-agile-project-managerthe-essence-of-agile-metrics.html

# Chapter 4 – Pillar #3:

# Cross-Functional Team Practices

After a cursory glance, I can see people easily thinking that this is the least important of the Three Pillars. Everyone seems to gravitate to the more tactical automation, tooling, and testing practices with their organizational quality and testing efforts. They're certainly easier to understand and execute, while also seeming to drive the largest ROI. In a word, they are more tangible and easier to grasp.

But, I've found that this pillar holds the most promise for your efforts. It's the most "Agile" of all of the pillars because it focuses on the individual and the team; in other words, it's about the people. That's the first thing you need to understand about agility in general. For example, when you're selecting tools, you should focus less on the tools and more on how the tools help the teams do better work. Ask your team what they think about them and what they need to get their job done.

The other side of this pillar, and I'm not sure if they are emphasized enough, are the agile principles. This pillar is principle-based. For example, this is where the team should be considering the four core tenants of the Agile Manifesto and its twelve underlying principles. There should be ongoing and passionate discussion surrounding them. This is also where team professionalism and craftsmanship resides. Where pride in the work and the craft of software development are not just words, but in fact, underscore all aspects of each team's daily focus.

## *It Takes...Courage*

Speaking of principles and values, the five core Scrum values have been defined as:

1. Commitment
2. Openness
3. Focus
4. Respect
5. **Courage**

While all five are important, I've always felt that agile team members require <u>courage</u> on a daily basis; this is even more important for quality and testing focused team members. For example:

- It takes <u>courage</u> to challenge the customer as to whether they truly need functionality as requested;
- It takes <u>courage</u> to explain to developers that a 2-point story is actually 10-points because of the testing implications;
- It takes <u>courage</u> to bring up Scrummer-fall behaviors in a retrospective, and to demand improved swarming and teamwork across your team;
- It takes <u>courage</u> to "fight for" the repair of some significant, but not high priority, bugs because of the potential impact they have on customer satisfaction;
- It takes <u>courage</u> to trust new, untried, and risky ideas that your team comes up with—particularly when you're in "crunch mode";
- Furthermore, it takes <u>courage</u> to leverage a balanced Three Pillars view towards your agile testing and quality transformation—seeing things through to high-performance and value delivery.

Hopefully, the spirit and focus of this chapter is already coming through. It's about the people, trust, craft and professionalism, doing the right things right, and having courage. In effect, this is the pillar that connects to the foundation, glues the other pillars together and activates your agile transformation strategies.

## *Stopping the Line*

One more fundamental part of the courage proposition is being willing, able, and firm in "stopping the line" when you encounter impediments and/or opportunities for improvement. This stop-the-line mentality just doesn't apply to software or your products. It applies to every aspect of how your teams and your organizations play. Let me share a personal example:

---

*I've been leading technology teams for many years. For example, if a team member leaves the company, I want to know why. I also want to know the root cause, and then immediately try and figure out how to prevent that from happening again. Often, I will stop-the-line amongst my leadership team and explore the 'why' behind the departure.*

*I also don't hide this introspection from the broader team. I want them to know that I care about the team, their morale, and attrition. In addition, I want them to understand that as a leadership team, we take every departure seriously, as seriously as each new-hire we bring aboard. While I know this is more of a leadership driven example, it's the intentionality that I wanted to amplify.*

*If encountering something "wrong" or "broken", every team member needs to have the courage to stop-the-line – even if it might be a false alarm, or something really hard to face. This stop-inspect-improve mentality is one of the core principles at the center of agility. In other words, each of us needs a relentless and courageous focus on continuous improvement.*

---

Now, to wrap up this introductory section, I think Mary's story surrounding team trust is a great indicator of another principle-based focus within our agile teams.

## Mary's Corner

*One of my favorite stories comes from the 5 Dysfunctions of a team training that occurred with my QA team at iContact. Before we ever got to the training event, the consultancy sent all the members of the team a survey around the 5 Dysfunctions. Being a little egocentric, I thought that out of all the teams, my QA team should score the best. They should trust each other because whom else would they trust—you can't trust developer's right? My team above all others did not fear conflict; heck they loved it. They were as committed as any QA team that I had ever had. They were accountable and were driven by results. We were going to ace this. In my mind we really didn't even need the training.*

*Let's just say I was sadly mistaken.*

*We did not have the best, nor worst results, but we had a lot to work on. We immediately dove into the results and which category was the worst offender...the foundational one...TRUST. Testers trusted the other testers on their Scrum team, but they did not trust the other testers on other Scrum teams and what they tested. It made no sense to me. I naively asked how could this be?*

*Then one of the members said, " Mary, our Scrum team is like our "street gang", We spend 39 hours a week with them, and 1 hour a week with, what I would call, "my family" – the other members of the QA team. To be able to survive, many times we have to go along with the gang even though we want to do what is right for the "family".*

*To this day, this is my favorite analogy of how matrix QA works in Scrum. There is much work you need to do to make sure you carry out team building events, and to make sure that the "family" sticks together -- as well as the teams. Always remember to continue to focus on building TRUST deeply and broadly.*

*Figure 9* provides an overview of the focus for this pillar. Next, I'll be drilling into some of the key areas of Pillar Three. I hope it proves to be an interesting journey.

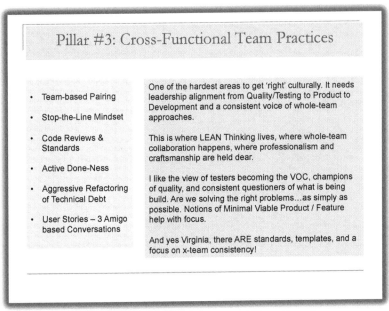

Figure 9, Pillar #3 – Cross-Functional Team Practices

## *Teaming*

On the surface, I think most organizations spend too little thought and effort towards the logistics of setting up or establishing agile teams. They often just "throw a group" of individuals together and expect them to behave like a team. Then, everyone is shocked and disappointed when this doesn't happen; imagine that?

I believe there's more to teaming than that and I want to spend a little time discussing it. When I think of effective agile teams, the following comes to mind:

- The team is as co-located as possible given the organizational constraints. If team members are in the same building, they sit together. If they're distributed, they have the facilities (tools, applications, phone, camera's, etc.) to effectively collaborate on day one.

- The team is committed to collaboration independent of their distribution.
- The team has gone through a team introductory exercise where they've gotten to know each other, established a team vision, and team norms. In Scrum, the Scrum Master would facilitate this.
- The team discusses breaking down silos in their work.
- The team augments the organizations Definition-of-Done and makes it their own.
- The team commits to working hard, having fun, and striving for continuous improvement via reflection.
- Finally, the team commits to congruent and transparent communication across the team.

## Stories – Teaming Matters!

### Norms

I wrote a blog post about the importance of roles and responsibilities in agile teams. There's a link to it in the references at the end of the chapter. Here's a snippet from that post about a Scrum Master who focused on establishing norms—

---

*Do we need roles and responsibility clarity in agile teams? I hope the answer is a clear and firm – Yes.*

*I think you owe your teams this as a Scrum Master and coach. That even the best of us often forget how important "starting up well" is. One of our more senior Scrum Masters at iContact reminded me of this when she joined our team. Her name was Maureen Green.*

*Maureen came in and found that her team hadn't established team norms and agreements, that they hadn't made our organizational Definition-of-Done their own, and that they were waffling on many of the principles we aspired to hold firm to. Instead of just charging forward, she "paused" her team and established these sorts of agreements and clarity first. Not only that, she served as a role model for our other Scrum Masters to tighten things up in this important area.*

*If you're struggling with your teams' execution and results, I would encourage you to consider "starting over" and redefining your agreements and principles as a way to accelerate forward.*

## Co-location & WIP

I once was coaching a team that was really struggling to deliver on their sprint commitments. They failed about 3-4-5 sprints in a row – delivering around 60-70% of what they had planned. They tried some trivial adjustments based on retrospective feedback, but they were in a vicious cycle of continuous failure.

I wrote a blog post about this experience and, what I did as their coach to free them from the cycle. It was simple really; I recommended two things to them:

*First, I asked them to co-locate and sit together as a team – to find a place where they could all sit together for just one sprint. I spoke about the quintessential agile team environment, where everyone sat at a long table along both sides. The entire team sitting in a single room, where they could see and hear each other and where they would be naturally pairing. A room where they could pull away from their laptops and gather around a whiteboard, and where they could have their daily Scrum right in the same space. Could they just try it...for only a 2-week sprint?*

*Next, I asked them to limit their work-in-progress or WIP. I did not necessarily have a "magic number", but I thought that a WIP limit of three might be useful for them. The team could only work on three user stories in the sprint backlog at one time. These would be the highest priority stories. In order for them to pick up the next story, they would have to complete one of the current three, and then demonstrate that it met their Definition-of-Done.*

Long story short, these simple adjustments, based on core principles of solid agile team behavior, broke them out of their dysfunction. In fact, in their very first sprint, they delivered two times what they had previously been delivering.

I encourage you to read the entire post and visit the link in the references at the end of the chapter. But, the real point I'm making is that collaboration, swarming, and teamwork really matters. Please focus on it in your adoption efforts.

## *The Three Amigo's*

Do you recall the story I told in the very beginning of the book? It described an organization that inspired the whole Three Pillars approach. In a nutshell, the organization was focusing too heavily on Cucumber-based BDD test automation development, while struggling with writing the simplest of user stories. In effect, they were unbalanced. They also didn't quite understand the connection between user stories and acceptance criteria or related BDD tests.

George Dinwiddie is the "father" of the Three Amigo's idea when it comes to user stories. In fact, let's generalize the concept to covering the interactions over any agile requirements. George established the metaphor for agile work being best represented by three constituents—

1.  **The Developer:** who represents the technical aspects, things like architecture, design, workflow and level of effort. They bring a sense of development "goodness" to the table in the discussions, for example, building things right from their perspective.

2.  **The Tester:** who represents doing things right, as well. However, in this case, right is nuanced towards functional and non-functional requirements. Another part of the concern is; are we building the "right thing"? There is a natural connection to the customer. In many ways, the tester is the fulcrum in the Three Amigos – sitting between developer and customer.

3.  **The Business or the Customer:** who represents the business case for a feature and ultimately how it will be used. They also define the behavior with the guidance of the developers and

testers. Another aspect, which is crucial within agile teams, is that they accept the work by establishing conditions of acceptance for it.

Think of this <u>Three Amigo's relationship</u> as being core to the pairing dynamics within mature agile teams.

An extension of this concept is the notion of a Three Amigo's meeting where these constituencies have a more formal meeting to discuss their stories. Often, this meeting is during backlog refinement and right before the story is worked in a sprint. I know quite a few teams who look at their agile workflow as a series of stories that need to be refined towards their sprint execution. They will conduct Three Amigo's meetings on a story-by-story basis as the sole mechanism for refining the stories.

## Mary's Corner

*For me this notion of the Three Amigo's has always been key. Before it was coined as the Three Amigo's, it was also described as the Power of Three. I always tell my QA teams that if you see a Product Owner and developer talking, you need to go and involve yourself in the conversation. I tell them to do this until it becomes a habit within the team. I love it when the Product Owner and developers are discussing relevant story work and they naturally include the tester closest to them.*

*An interesting event happened to me at a company where I was working. I had a tester who would grab me almost daily to discuss how many meetings the Product Owner was having with the developers and not including him. I asked if he went over and joined the conversations? He said that he did not as it felt like he was intruding. Also, the PO was long winded and, more often than not, wasted people's time.*

*After every conversation, I encouraged him to partner more with the Product Owner. To insert himself in the conversations, and to figure out what they were discussing. Several sprints went by and not much changed. I would walk by the team pods and still see the Product Owner only talking to developers without any testers. When it finally came time to release to production, this particular tester had some legitimate concerns about the release. The problem was it was now too late to communicate with them. He tried, but he had never built a relationship with the PO, so when all the developers on the team said everything was fine, the tester's cry was met by deaf ears.*

*After the release, the QA engineer came back to me for more advice. He said," You know I think I get it now...He (the Product Owner) did not TRUST me because we rarely communicated." I said, "Exactly!" The conversations you have with the PO and the developers build trust so that when there are legitimate concerns, everyone will listen. That's what the Three Amigo's means – three different viewpoints all with same amount of respect and weight.*

*After that day, that tester was in almost every Product Owner and developer side conversation that he saw; this made a huge difference when it came to the next release. The QA Engineer had expressed his concerns to the Product Owner and developers throughout the sprints and, therefore, when the tester expressed those concerns at release time, everyone took action to mitigate them. Everyone appreciated and understood the concerns...there were no deaf ears!*

## *The Evolution of Pair Programming*

Pair-Programming was introduced as an Extreme Programming (XP) practice by Kent Back around 2000. Originally, it was very programming and programmer-centric. It was also viewed as a "mandatory" practice – in that <u>all code</u> was written in pairs.

Today, pairing is much more of a general-purpose technique within agile teams. The mandatory nature has softened towards more of an <u>opportunistic pairing</u> approach. And from developer-centric it's moved to more of a team-centric model, in that all members of the team can and should randomly pair.

Now, with the Three Amigos mindset, it's even more generic. I want pairs, triads, and even small groups collaborating around building customer code. That is from the first time a group picks up a user story to implement within a sprint, until the Product Owner signs-off on that story as being complete. There should be tight collaboration, discussion, and demonstration going on amongst the amigos for that story.

## Amigo's – Beyond the "Story"

Furthermore, before you get stuck on the notion that the amigos only interact on stories during their sprint execution, don't. The interactions happen during release planning, story creation, backlog refinement, and even during the sprint retrospective.

The analogy is one of role-based, collaborative interaction, consistently and constantly, across the team. It honors the roles that everyone brings to the table, and amplifies that interaction across those roles is what creates excellent and valuable work.

# Definition-of-Done (DoD)

A good place to go next is drilling into more specifics of a Definition-of-Done or Done-Ness Criteria. Consider done-ness to be the "rules" that constrain the teams' work. If the team were building a bridge, then it would be the engineering rules, practices, inspection steps, local regulations, and completion requirements that would permeate everything the build team would do. In many ways, the Definition-of-Done should seep into every aspect of your agile team's collaboration.

For a long time, I've been a strong proponent of a 4-layered view to done-ness. In this view, these layers build upon one another, moving from individual-based work, to story-based work, to sprint-based work, and ultimately, to a release. I often use the term _guardrails_ to indicate the guideline nature of the criteria in guiding the teams' efforts.

Now let's review the four levels:

1. **Work Product:** This is the layer of the individual contributor. For example, your front-end developers should define some rules, conventions, and standards for how they design and develop, test and deliver their UI code. The adherence to these standards should be defined specifically as done-ness criteria. This same logic applies to each functional role within the agile team. Everyone should define a set of constraints that surrounds professional delivery of their work products.

2. **Story Level:** This is the work delivery level. If you're using user stories, then done-ness in this context would define a rich and meaningful set of *acceptance tests* per story; then holding yourselves accountable to delivering to those functional constraints. Remember, acceptance tests are incredibly useful as design aids and test aids when the team is sorting out the nuance of each story. One of the most important parts of the acceptance tests are the business logic design hints they can provide.

    You should also develop clear quality goals at this level. It may sound prescriptive, but I like all bugs that have been found in the development of a story to be fixed prior to declaring that story complete. These aren't legacy bugs, but bugs created and found during the development of the story. I can't tell you how many times teams run into problems at the end of the sprint in delivering a completely done story. Usually it's because they haven't left sufficient time to completely finish the work they took on. Often this indicates a collaboration issue, i.e. they simply took on too much parallel work.

3. **Sprint-Level Criteria or Sprint Goal(s):** This level is focused towards how well the team met all of the criteria they set forth when planning their sprint. A large part of this is focused towards having a successful sprint review or demo. Think of "connecting the dots" between the sprint goal and the sprint review; the team should view the goal as a cohesive demonstration of business value from the customers point of view.

I often get asked if a sprint can have multiple goals, i.e. deliver on multiply focused activities. The answer is probably yes, but what the question is really looking for is the ability to say:

> *The goal of this sprint is to deliver 524 hours of work towards these specific 12 User Stories that are sized at 27 Story Points.*

I think this is an incredibly poor goal because of the tactical, work effort focus. There is no "customer" or no "demo description" in the goal. I would much prefer goals that have a clear connection to the customer, value, and challenges embedded within the goal. Having two to three separate goals articulated in this way seems fine as well.

4.  **Release-Level Criteria or Release Goal(s):** If you've ever been part of a team that delivered software in more waterfall environments, a common practice is to create *release criteria*. These are more holistic requirements that are usually established at the beginning, or early on, in a project. Often, they are consistent from project to project or release to release, because they quantify organizationally important criteria. For example, quantifying whether you could release with specific levels of bugs (both in priority and count) or quantifying how much testing (coverage percentage) is needed to occur prior to a release.

    One of the unfortunate parts of many agile adoptions is that these sorts of criteria have been skipped or dropped. I believe them to be incredibly valuable in defining meta-requirements or key constraints for the teams to adhere to within each release. Typically, they exist anyway within the organization, but calling them out creates a focus on them in planning, execution, and delivery. They're particularly important in at-scale delivery so that multiple teams are maintaining a consistent focus on the overall release goals.

## Getting Done-Ness Into Your DNA

Creating a list of your done-ness criteria is only the first step. Just because you have created and communicated them, doesn't mean that everyone is supporting them. The next step is establishing a culture where everyone aligns with and personally supports the criteria. Not just when things are going smoothly, but also when the going gets tough.

You know that your done-ness has seeped into your culture when the team sees no other recourse but to do things the right way. I'll share this example from iContact that nicely illustrates this cultural transformation:

*iContact built a SaaS e-mail marketing product that our customers used 7x24. In fact, our weekends were often quite busy as SMB[16] owners worked on their next week's email campaigns. There was one weekend where a nasty mail sending component bug cropped up. It brought down our ability to send email, which clearly affected all of our clients. Not only that, when this happened, we would queue the mail. This started to create an endlessly increasing pool of mail that would cause huge delays even after we fixed the bug.*

*Needless to say, the pressure was on.*

*Our teams would normally assign a "support engineer" for weekend support work. The engineer in this case was notified of the problem, looked into it, and devised a repair. As part of our DoD, we'd agreed that no fix or repair could be checked-in without a paired code review. Now, keep in mind—this was a holiday weekend, so people were on vacation. The support engineer determined that he needed a review with two others who were experienced in this area of the mail-sending stack.*

*He located them via text messages and phone calls and they all committed to a distributed/remote code review session on Saturday afternoon. They discussed a few issues and changes related to the repair, which he completed before releasing the repair.*

---

[16] Small to Medium Sized Business

*When I came in on Monday morning, I was amazed at how committed the team was to doing a proper review. It would have been the easiest thing in the world to have either checked-in an un-reviewed repair OR, waited until everyone was back on Monday. However, the support engineer and his team were committed to our customers and to our Definition-of-Done. It was in their DNA.*

## Mary's Corner

*One of the first questions I ask my QA group when I join a new organization is whether they can recite their doneness criteria? Incredibly often, nobody can.*

*The reason I ask this question is because, in my opinion, testers should champion this, own it, keep everyone accountable for it, be courageous, and ask the hard questions surrounding it. I have found when they do this, and they really own/champion understanding their doneness criteria, the quality of the releases are much better and, therefore, and the whole-team starts to get on board.*

## *Attacking Technical Debt*

The idea of Technical Debt might be one of the greatest gifts that the agile community has given us. Prior to the agile movement, we largely ignored the costs associated with infrastructure, tooling, refactoring/redesign, and bug upkeep, within our products. All of those are mostly from a software development point of view. But, it's incredibly useful to get the idea "on the table" for discussion, and negotiation, with more feature-driven work for our projects. For far too long, we've starved these areas and our product quality and our customers have suffered as a result.

In an article I wrote about a year ago (see reference section), I extended technical debt to include testing centric gaps. For example, I included tests that are not run within the iteration or sprint due to planning or other factors, as an aspect of Technical Test Debt. These are coverage gaps that probably need to be closed in a later sprint. Often risk-based testing techniques create these gaps. I consider it healthy testing behavior to have this level of thinking within each sprint.

But there is an incremental danger of releasing a product without fully testing it. In fact, in regulated environments, this would cause legal liability concerns as well, and that's just one aspect of technical test debt. There are others, for example, test automation that has been left to decay without proper upkeep. So, please read the article and when you think of technical debt, don't just think about if from an architectural or development perspective, think about ongoing quality and testing debts as well.

## *Aggressive Refactoring of Technical Debt*

I teach many classes surrounding the agile methods. By doing that, I often get challenged concerning agile in the "Real World". Believe it or not, everyone isn't falling all over himself or herself to adopt agility properly. A commonly occurring story follows:

---

*In my Product Owner classes, I try to influence the attendees to take an "all work" view when constructing their product backlogs. What I mean by that is too many teams think that only features reside on the backlog. All the "other stuff" they need to do is somehow magically completed before they release the software. I struggle with this approach of assuming work will get done, particularly if that work is necessary to stage the features for the customer.*

*My preferred view is to get <u>all work</u> necessary to deliver a release on the product backlog to make it more visible and to make the trade-offs and the costs clear. If the team decides to skip something, then the risks are also clear. For example:*

- *Infrastructure work; including development, testing, architecture, whatever;*
- *Bug fixes; enhancement requests;*
- *Refactoring work; cleanup or stabilization work;*
- *Investigative work – sometimes called Research Spikes or User Story Spikes; often producing prototype code;*
- *Testing activities or phases;*
- *Equipment and tooling setup; not minor nits, but major activities;*

- *Training and teambuilding;*
- *Agile project chartering activity.*

*One of the challenges with this view is cost justifying these elements versus the features on the backlog. It seems as if most Product Owners don't really care about this "extra stuff". From their perspective, it doesn't provide customer-facing value so, while it's probably important, they don't want to hear about it.*

*Nonetheless, this work is crucial for creating quality and stable products. I highly recommend taking this approach and, if you meet resistance, you'll need to create strategies for introducing this sort of approach.*

---

## Empowered for Technical Debt

In general, agile teams need to be empowered to place technical debt, refactoring, and infrastructural work actively on their backlogs, which is often rather hard to do. I've seen two somewhat dysfunctional patterns that you'll want to avoid. Either:

1. Teams will tend to place <u>everything</u> related to technical debt on the product backlog. Literally, hundreds of discrete items. This has the effect of <u>freezing</u> the Product Owner from making any decisions because of the sheer volume of requests. A related problem is the team doesn't justify the need for the technical debt items in business or ROI terms. They simply throw them on the backlog and expect them to get done without justification.

2. The other pattern is the reverse. Usually, because they've become disillusioned or because nobody has paid attention to their historical requests for technical debt work, the team stops making the case altogether. They view the business as not caring or understanding their plight, as the software gets harder and harder to maintain and deliver.

## Approaches That Seem to Work

Probably the most powerful, or healthy approach for this is to simply handle the teams backlog feedback on an as needed basis. The team explains and justifies the work, the Product Owner prioritizes it, and they steadily address their technical debt. Some sprints would have more and others less, as the team works together to sort out a healthy balance between feature work and technical debt work.

Unfortunately, this rarely seems to happen in the real world of many agile teams. In these contexts, the Product Owners often ignore the debt for long periods of time. If this is your situation, another approach is to establish guidelines for technical debt percentages within the backlog. Usually these are applied on a broad basis, sprint-by-sprint and for the overall release.

For example, at iContact we agreed to an *80/20 split* [17]in new features versus technical debt in our product backlog work balance. In fact, we were quite strict about the percentage so that teams understood how serious we were about our product investment mix. It was also part of our release planning and embedded within our release goals. Even with this strong support, it was difficult for us to influence the teams to contribute story candidates for this work. They had become so accustomed to ignoring technical debt, that it took quite a while for them to realize how committed we were to attacking it.

Salesforce has a unique and powerful approach that they shared in a 2010 Agile Conference presentation. It went like this:

---

*If any team hasn't achieved 70% automated coverage of their legacy code base, then a penalty is exacted. In addition to any technical debt that is already on their Product Backlog, an additional 20% of the backlog is replaced with automation development work to bring them up to that 70% goal. This goal, or criteria, comes from the top down and is non-negotiable.*

---

It implies a couple of key points that I want to amplify. First, Salesforce's understanding at a leadership level that in order for agile teams to "go fast", they need automated testing in place. The second point is that

---

[17] The 80/20 mix was something that we ended up with. We oscillated around 10% - 25% of our investments for Technical Debt. In our case, we rolled legacy defect repairs into this percentage as well. Another point, our sprints rarely perfectly hit the percentages, but we always het the targets on a release basis.

leadership didn't simply <u>say</u> that technical debt was important; they put their money where their mouth was and <u>supported it</u>. Very few organizations have the agile maturity to take this strong a stance, so I really admire their conviction.

There's another subtler side effect. This message permeates into other areas of the Salesforce culture. What leadership is saying is that they want to do agile properly. They want to deliver the right thing and then, do it right. That message pays dividends in activating the empowerment of their teams.

## Mary's Corner

*To that point Bob, your QA Leadership should have a Test Technical Debt roadmap that you work towards, and expose transparently, to the whole organization. At iContact, when we got all our tests Green for the first time, Bob bought beer for everyone at a Town hall meeting.*

*Another approach that I have seen work well is leveraged within retrospectives. I have them with the entire Scrum team; we place Post-it Notes on the whiteboard for all our QA and Development technical debt items. It's a whole-team view towards quality in which I have found that the developers had some of the best ideas to attack the debt.*

*I also have a quarterly retrospective with just my QA team. I do this to get a collective view across the organization and to see which pillars we are falling short on. I then create quarterly goals just for the QA team to try and improve in the respective areas.*

## *Wrapping Up*

Creating truly self-directed teams is a central component of agile's success. That's why I love it when folks challenge me on agility and whether it will work in the "real world". It's like, OK, what part of trusting, enabling, empowering, and energizing your teams don't you like? I simply don't get it. Yes, there are many agile methods and a myriad of tactics and tools, but ultimately the success of agile in your organization boils down to you and how well you inspire and activate your people.

For example, a sprint retrospective can either be by rote or incredibly powerful. If your teams are accountable for continuous improvement and driving results, then they'll creatively and innovatively adjust to improve on these fronts. It also leverages cross-functional teamwork.

And not a façade of teamwork, but instead, true teamwork that genuinely drives continuous collaboration, high-energy and excitement, as well as, high-impact results. There's a book by James Surowiecki called the *Wisdom of Crowds*, where he makes the case of the power of the "crowd", in this case the team, over any single individual. This applies even to individuals who appear to have super-human intellect or coding ability.

Ultimately, that's what "going Agile" is trying to do – activate the awesome power of your teams. Within the context of this pillar and chapter, testing and quality focused team members play an incredibly important part in that <u>activation</u>.

## *References*

- Core Scrum Principles:
  - o a blog post by Mike Vizdos here:
    http://www.implementingscrum.com/2008/03/25/scrum-values-learn-them-live-them/
  - o And you can see them articulated on the Scrum Alliance site here:
    http://www.scrumalliance.org/pages/code_of_ethics
- George Dinwiddie –
  - o InfoQ interview:
    http://www.infoq.com/interviews/george-dinwiddie-three-amigos
  - o 3 Amigos Stickyminds article
    http://www.stickyminds.com/sitewide.asp?Function=edetail&ObjectType=COL&ObjectId=17232
- James Surowiecki called the *Wisdom of Crowds*
- Blog post about Roles and Responsibilities –
  http://rgalen.com/agile-training-news/2014/4/14/roles-and-responsibilities-do-we-need-such-things-for-agile-teams
- Blog post about Co-location & Teaming –
  http://rgalen.com/agile-training-news/2013/3/9/the-agile-project-manager-wipping-things-into-shape.html

# Chapter 5 – Crossing Pillars:

# Agile Transformation Strategies

I've been waiting to dig into this chapter for quite a while. This is where the real value of the Three Pillars resides – considering crosscutting values while crafting your agile testing adoption strategy. So, what are the dimensions of this strategy? In order to make the point, perhaps we can explore three anti-patterns of effective agile testing adoption. I see all of them fairly often in my travels and think that establishing what not to do might be a good way to begin this chapter.

## *Anti-Pattern: Testing Goes Away*

In this case, the strategy is that you need few to no testers, or narrow testing, within the agile methods. The intent, as I've mentioned before, comes from the early days of the methods, mostly because of their developer-driven emphasis. The other driver for it is the "generalist" view that many have in the agile community. That instead of specialized skills, everyone can do every job within the team. This not only impacts testers, but also development roles, for example, front-end versus backend development. Those views still percolate today and cause many teams to literally forget about the testing team when they're "going Agile".

Now, I'm not implying that the testers are fired, although that often happens. Instead, I'm simply saying that testing is marginalized even more than it normally is. Processes are dropped and testing becomes functionally driven at a story level. Automation may be created, but it is entirely developer-centric. Test leadership is stuck trying to guide their testers through a sea of agile so that they do work, but make as few waves as possible.

There are many examples of companies who physically reframe the tester role, essentially removing it, as part of their agile adoption: Google, Microsoft, and Facebook are well known and documented examples of this thinking. I consider this strategy (or lack thereof) an anti-pattern, however, it does set the stage for what not to do. Let's explore another.

## Anti-pattern: Testing Goes On

Another frequent strategy is changing virtually nothing. This often happens in regulated, or mission-critical, environments. Generally, the logic is that all of the testing practices, tactics, measures, and approaches <u>must</u> stay the same. Then, there is a litany of reasons of why—for the regulators, for the auditors, for the Project Management Office, of accounting practices, to support the "Software Process".

Now, there is a "grain of truth" in all of these claims. Typically, these environments are less then supportive of the iterative testing tempo that agile requires. They also struggle with the entire agile requirements process. That being said, not changing at all, is a recipe for disaster.

My favorite story that illustrates this is from a large organization that I coached a few years ago:

---

*They was a large Scrum agile instance of 100-120 Scrum teams. At the time, they had a testing organization of about 300-350 testers supporting over a 1000 developers. When the testing leadership decided to "go Agile", they reserved about 300 of their testers to continue running integration, system, and regression testing, as they'd always done it. Some of these tests were automated, but the majority of them were manual— approximately a 20/80 split. These tests needed a tremendous amount of "care and feeding".*

*That left approximately 50 testers, in reality about 30, to be integrated with their Scrum teams. Also, if you're doing the ratio based math – that was one tester for every three Scrum teams. Clearly, the testers on the Scrum teams were overloaded to the point of ineffectiveness. This was even more troubling since the traditional testing team was moving slowly in their test preparation and execution.*

*But, the insidious problem with this ratio imbalance was that the agile testers had no time to feed the traditional team the change specifications*

*for new work. They simply didn't have the time to collaborate with the
Scrum teams and pass along the information to the regression crew.
Therefore, over time, the tests became more and more stale or invalid. In
order to get them caught up, the testers had to rework their tests outside
of the iterative model – thus slowing things down.*

*In the end, this model proved to be 30-40% slower than their Waterfall
equivalent in delivering software. They were incredibly out of balance. It
turned out that the "right" ratio was nearly the reverse of their initial
investment; that is 300 testers scattered across the Scrum teams, and 50
held in reserve to run the larger-scale testing cycles. Once they had
switched the ratios, and began to truly support their Scrum teams, things
worked surprisingly well.*

## Mary's Corner

*Bob, I know you hate ratios, but you have to have them in nearly every
organization. If you have a new team and no test automation – I like the
2:1 ratio since there is much work to be done from the automation setup
perspective. Once you have 200-300 tests, or until you have a fairly low
maintenance test suite, then I like the ratio of 3:1, but that is absolutely as
low as I will go.*

## *Anti-pattern: Unbalanced - Drill Down*

I exposed a variant of this anti-pattern in the book's Introduction. The
primary focus here is to pick a few agile testing practices and then focus
on them to the exclusion of everything else. Often, this "feels good" and I
often hear it defined as a "taking baby steps" pattern. The problem with
it is two-fold:

1. Many times the organization and teams pick the agile practices
   that are easiest to implement in their culture. Sometimes these
   are the right things to focus on, but more often, they're not.

2. Balance is lost. Most, if not all of the agile principles, are interlocking and interrelated. That implies that it's hard to take a
   piecemeal approach. Sure, you don't have to accelerate across

20 practices equally, but you do have to create an interlocking strategy in order to largely gain the benefits of agility.

Here's a snippet from the Introduction that illustrated this anti-pattern:

---

*One of the things I noticed is that the firm had gone "all in" on Behavior-Driven Development (BDD) leveraging Cucumber as the tooling framework. They had invited in several consultants to teach courses to many of their Scrum teams and everyone got "test infected"[18]. Teams were literally creating thousands of BDD level automated tests in conjunction with delivering their software. From their perspective, there was incredible energy and enthusiasm. Everyone contributed tests while measuring the number of increasing Cucumber tests on a daily basis.*

*However, a few days into my coaching, I was invited to a backlog grooming session where a team was writing and developing their user stories. What I expected was to simply be an observer. What actually happened is that I quickly realized the team didn't know how to write a solid user story. They could barely write one at all. On their request, I ended up delivering an ad-hoc user story writing class for them. Afterwards, the team was incredibly appreciative as they started to understand the important place that solid story writing held in the agile development lifecycle.*

*Over the next few days, I realized something very important. The organization was at two levels when it came to their agile quality and testing practices. Either they were <u>all in</u>, or they were <u>unaware of, or under-practicing</u> specific techniques. For example, they were all in on BDD and writing automated Cucumber tests and on Continuous Integration; however, they struggled mightily with simply writing user stories and, literally, had no clear or consistent Definition-of-Done.*

---

[18] To use a term coined by Elizabeth Hendrickson – http://testobsessed.com/

Now that I've established some "don't do this" strategies; let's explore more effective approaches for morphing your quality and testing strategies towards agile methods. I've already let one key factor out of the bag—believing that a "balanced" approach between your established testing techniques and agile techniques is required.

Let's call it a "balanced transformation" to agile quality. As we move through this chapter, keep in mind the basic Three Pillars framework and the foundational practices from Chapter 1. You might even want to print them out. That should help you visualize and embed better balance as you develop your agile quality and testing strategies.

## What Do I Mean By "Strategy"?

Before I go much further, it's probably best to establish a baseline understanding of what I mean by strategy. When my co-conspirator, Mary Thorn, and I worked together at iContact, she did a wonderful job of establishing and running with an agile quality and testing strategy within her QA organization. Mary reported to me and was the director of our testing team. We would periodically sit down to discuss the overall agile strategy I envisioned for the organization and then drill into the quality and testing bits that she would need to support.

I had the overall "Big Picture", and I expected Mary to develop a quality-centric view that integrated with our overall organizational plans. We would iterate on this several times until we had a synchronized view between us. Then Mary would align and rationalize her quality goals with her team. Yes, I said it, with her team. She would meet with the entire group and share her vision. However, together they would build a roadmap of specific activities geared towards realizing that vision.

This transition looked very much like the one made from release planning activity as organizations move from roadmaps to product backlogs. But, as in release planning, the results went far beyond the plans themselves. What they were creating was a shared vision, a shared strategy, and a shared view, to the path to get there. We considered several steps necessary to establish and execute a strategy. At a high level, I'll explore those steps next.

## *Begin with the End in Mind – Goals*

As I said, Mary would sit down with me and brainstorm the quality and testing goals that we wanted to establish across our organization. There were three key things that we considered while doing this:

1. **Balance across the Three Pillars** – At the time we hadn't defined the pillars, so we were going merely by instinct and good judgment. Now, that we have articulated the model, it's easier to see where we might be missing something. In our practice, we tried very hard to balance across principles, tactics, and across functions, for example, development vs. testing vs. architecture.

2. **Compelling or BHAG** – We wanted the goals to be reasonable and achievable. But, at the same time, we wanted them to be compelling. There's the notion of a Big Hairy Audacious Goal, or BHAG, and that truly represents our intentions towards goal setting. Also, goals were at different levels; we had annual roadmap goals that were connected to quarterly and annual organizational goals.

3. **Integrated with our overall Agile Transformation Strategy** – This is where Mary and I needed to create a shared vision for our overall agile transformation and then explore the quality and testing bits. The implication here was cross-functional, cross-team, and cross-organizational strategic vision—no silos allowed.

Remember, goals are rarely "for" leadership. Leadership establishes them, connects them, strategizes them, and measures them; but the goals are <u>for the team</u>. They should promote action and excitement.

They should inspire creativity and innovation towards meeting them – something beyond by-rote execution, but instead providing the inspiration towards the "essence" of each goal.

## *Organizational Integration*

It is the norm in most non-agile organizations to construct your strategies and goals around functional silos. Sure, there might be some crosscutting goals at a very high level, for example, to meet some esoteric cost savings targets. But in general, goals are defined by the test teams' leadership for testing teams, and similarly for the development teams, and so on. It is purely a functional activity.

Within an agile organization, this needs to fundamentally change. That's what I've alluded to in the third point above. Yes, the testing organization should define, refine, and execute on their strategies. However, they need to be integrated cross-functionally so that everyone on the teams are working together and focused essentially on the same goals.

For example, the testers cannot implement user stories as a new requirement medium without it being a <u>whole-team</u> initiative. The training, driving forces, ultimate intentions, and goals surrounding this initiative, needs to cross all teams. Sure, the test organization may be the clear leader of the initiative as an inspirational change agent, but it needs to be reinforced more holistically. It needs to become <u>everyone's</u> goal with very specific definition and responsibilities to boot.

Minimally, your strategies need to touch across:

- Project Management – Scrum Masters
- Architecture and Business Analysis
- Development
- Testing
- UX Design
- Product Team – Product Owners
- DevOps or Technical Operational Team(s)
- Documentation
- Customer Facing Operational Team(s)

I know this might sound daunting and risk becoming a significant time-sink, but this sort of integration is required. Normally, it's the job of the organizational agile champion to "connect the dots", as in the example where Mary would connect her strategy to my overall vision.

Whether I'm an internal leader and agile change agent, or an external coach, I try to inspire my teams with a vision that knows no silos or functional boundaries.

## Where Do Your "Strategic Plans" Reside?

I hate to tell you this, but you no longer have to write independent plans, at least not at a strategic level. Sure you might pull together a high-level set of thoughts on a PowerPoint deck, but the details – the tactical steps, the tasks, the work plans, the sequencing, the milestones, and even reporting out results is sort of done for you.

That is if you do two simple things: by writing user stories expressing your strategic plans and then, executing them in an iterative, transparent, agile fashion. Sort of eating our own agile dog food if you will.

By capturing your strategy efforts in user story format (or whatever container you're using to craft work on your backlogs) and working with your Product Owners to "feed" them to your teams, you'll be injecting:

- High-level work into your Product Roadmaps;
- As the stories are broken down, they'll surface in your Release Plans;
- As they're broken down into executable chunks, they'll be broken down for sprint execution;
- In addition, you'll see the results illustrated and discussed at each sprint review.

This natural process of story decomposition not only happens for "features", but it also happens for "initiative based work" such as your strategic plans. Essentially, the organizational leadership team becomes the Product Owner for agile transformation based strategic initiatives.

## Quarterly Planning & Progress

Agile tempo is a wonderful thing. I hope you've come to appreciate the value of truly time-boxed iterative development that delivers narrow slices of functionality on a regular basis. One of the advantages of the approach is the "heartbeat" it creates across the entire agile organization. Usually, there are two tempos that seep into your strategic planning:

1.  Sprint Tempo – the periodic delivery of "working software" that meets your Definition-of-Done and represents your agile teams' velocity for value delivery, and;

2.  Release Tempo – the periodic delivery of customer software. Software that is production environment based, and in-use by your customers. This is often represented by the term *Release Train*[19].

It's incredibly common to wrap your tactical steps towards your goals around your release tempo. That is, you plan for your strategy increments that overlap your release increments. Then progress is made towards these goals, on a sprint-by-sprint, and release-by-release basis.

I often look for the teams themselves to demonstrate strategic accomplishments in sprint reviews at the same level of importance that they do in their feature work. With this level of tempo-based progress, transparency is another side effect of taking this approach. After that, all you need to do is understand your strategy, attend the sprint reviews, and pay attention to progress and, of course, ask relevant questions as opportunities present themselves.

## Measures

As I mentioned in the last section, results should be transparent along sprint and release tempo boundaries. You'll want to set a tone of whole-team metrics, rather than measuring individual functional silos. In fact, measuring functional results is an anti-pattern in agile transformation

---

[19] This term originated with Dean Leffingwell and his agile scaling work. Now it's mostly referenced as part of the Scaled Agile Framework or SAFe. We also explored its origin's in the Pillar Two chapter.

because it leads to functional group sub-optimization rather than cross-team continuous improvement and results.

I also discussed at the end of the Pillar Two chapter, that metrics should generally surround four crucial areas: predictability, value delivered, quality, and team health. If you can, you should stop measuring all testing team and/or testing based activity. Here are a few guidelines for your team-based measurements:

1. Define quarterly goals that align with your Release Train model;
2. Measure progress to goal at a sprint level; use cross-team (organizational) information radiators to clearly expose progress;
3. Don't overreact to sprint-by-sprint fluctuations, as with velocity, average your progress over 2-3 Sprints. What's even more interesting is to consider trending of your measures.
4. Talk about progress to goal within each teams' sprint retrospective AND at a Scrum of Scrums level – adjusting accordingly;
5. Upon release, measure quarterly progress and baseline it;
6. Reflect on your goals, metrics, progress and results; then make adjustments as required;
7. Then rinse and repeat for your next release...

## Mary's Corner

*Here is a Three Pillars scorecard that I've used while working at a previous company. Just because I've evaluated the "Horizon" team at an "is doing" level in many areas, don't think they have little improvement work left to do. In fact, many of the is-doing areas need quite a lot of work. It's just that they're practicing them relatively consistently.*

*The real benefit of scorecards such as this are the discussions they drive in retrospectives and amongst the team. It serves as a baseline for evaluating and planning for continuous improvement.*

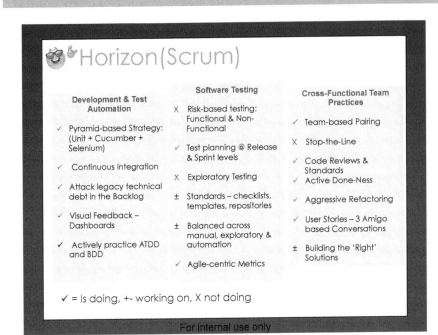

Figure 10, Example of Three Pillars Scorcard for a specific Scrum team

## *Reflection!*

I can't emphasize enough the importance of discussing your strategic initiatives within your team-based sprint and release level retrospectives. These are crucial ceremonies to keep your goals and progress <u>a focal point</u> for the entire organization.

You might even want to ask your Scrum Masters and teams to carve out a special section of each retrospective to discuss goals and progress for your agile transformations. This will give you solid information as to what's working, what's not, and ideas for strategy improvement.

It's probably a good practice to keep an information radiator or two that focus on just these areas, with data being generated in part from the retrospectives.

## Mary's Corner

*At iContact, we had a quarterly retrospective with the entire company. We would send out an anonymous survey, collate the results, and then discuss in retrospective style, the results. Many of our process improvement initiatives came from this. It was extremely valuable in that it made everyone feel like they had a voice.*

## Agile Strategies – In the Beginning

Next, I want to cover some "strategy snippets", or general-purpose guidelines, for establishing effective quality and testing focused agile adoption strategies. Some of them will be self-evident and others counterintuitive. Nonetheless, I've found these areas to be important considerations during my agile journey.

### Training

It's a common reaction for organizations to bring in general or overview agile training for teams moving towards agility. This usually includes an overview of various methods, agile requirements, and specific for roles such as Product Owner and/or Scrum Master. Often, two groups, Business Analysis and Testers, get left behind in the training.

A major reason for this is that most agile coaching and training firms have little experience with these niche roles. However, it's incredibly important to bring in training that couples agile testing, agile requirements, and agile quality dynamics—then running your whole team through them. Usually, you want to plan for this <u>before</u> you actually start sprinting.

### Definition-of-Done

One of the first questions Mary and I ask of new agile teams relates to their DoD. You'd be amazed how often the definition is something as shallow as: "the Product Owner signs-off on the Story"; which is all they have defined. While I consider that a part of done, I normally coach teams to have a very broad and deep set of done-ness criteria that they develop for their work, stories, sprints, and releases. This 4-level approach to DoD drives the collaboration and results that I feel are the hallmark of a solid agile team were discussed in the Pillar 3 chapter.

Additionally, you might ask who establishes them? Of course, it's an organizational and team focus, but I like to see the quality and testing folks serve as the inspiration for solid, broad, deep, and nuanced criteria – criteria that supports the promises of agile quality!

## Artifacts

The most common mistake that teams in transformation make is either stopping documentation all together or continuing to document everything as they always have. Both of these lead to a very poor transformations, although I see much more of the former in practice. The best strategy for a new team is typically two-fold:

1. **Leverage your existing artifacts**: Test plans, test design and case templates, defect templates, etc. The implication here is basically – always start from where you are. Don't throw everything out, and don't reinvent everything.

2. **But then, "agilify" everything**: I know that's not a word, but it does have meaning. I want you to slim everything down to its very essence. For each document, you need just enough of it to provide the inherent value. For example, a Test Plan is essentially a strategy document for the team. They are the audience and whole-team testing strategies developed in real-time are the goal. So, keep it short and focused on driving discussion and collaboration.

Another key is to embrace the emergent nature of agile requirements; i.e., the fact that everything is not defined in advance of execution. Become expert in user story writing, if that's what you're using for requirements.

## Tools

How many of you think that "leading with tools" is the right response in "going Agile"? Be honest. That's what I thought…about 90% of you think that tools are a critical early decision in your adoption efforts. By tools in this case, I'm implying testing-centric tooling as well as more generic agile planning (ALM) tooling. An incredibly common strategic pattern I see in adoption is the following:

1. Select a major vendor, identify and buy tool-sets;
2. Have the vendor help install/setup the tool and do team training;
3. Find a couple of Scrum Masters and Product Owners— overloading the roles is fine;
4. Tell the teams they're AGILE and to start coding/iterating immediately;
5. Sit back and wait to reap the benefits of agility...

In a word, "don't do that"! Remember the agile manifesto advice here regarding Individuals and Interactions (People and Collaboration) over Processes and Tools. While tools are important, especially in larger scale or distributed team environments, an overemphasis early on can lead to dysfunctional collaboration. I've literally seen this pattern over and over again.

Your strategy should be to install, or leverage, a very minimal set of just enough tools in the beginning of your agile adoption. Only what's absolutely necessary. Then over time, engage your teams in surfacing tool needs that map to your ongoing growth and agile needs. Get the whole-team involved in the effort and evolve your environments incrementally.

## Initial Metrics

In the beginning, it's important to connect to a very simple set of metrics that align with agile principles that will tell you how well your team is performing. Here's an example.
I like the notion of measuring 'escapes' as a quality metric. At iContact, we measured a handful of escape types:

1. **Sprint Escapes:** These were violations of our agile principles. For example, if a team ignored their DoD, then we would note that. If a feature or user story was delivered, but it wasn't completely done (even subtly), then we would call that an escape.

There could also be process-level escapes. For example, we agreed that every team would have a retrospective at the end of each sprint or that they would groom their backlogs twice a week. If a team broke one of these agreements or understandings, we would log it as a "process escape". There were no "magic numbers" as to what was acceptable in these cases. What we considered most important was to make the decisions transparent.

2.  **Defect Escapes:** These were bugs that escaped all of our testing efforts and landed in the lap of our customers. We would sample newly found bugs for a 2-week period after each of our production releases.

    If a customer found a new issue created by the release, we would log it as an escape. This would drive team activity around: root cause analysis, retrospective, and actions to prevent this escape from reoccurring. That might include more defensive programming, improved DoD, additional automation or other improvements.

3.  **Automated Test Cases:** In addition to escapes, we also felt that automation progress was important to measure. In this case, we differentiated the measures along the lines of the automation pyramid – measuring unit level, middle tier level, and UI level test automation as it evolved.

    We never drove with magic number targets or goals, instead measuring the trending sprint-over-sprint and release-over-release. What was important to us was that we were increasing our coverage and that it was driven by whole-team decision-making.

These were literally our only iContact quality metrics. While appearing quite simplistic, they drove all sorts of positive behavior and discussion and adaptation within our teams.

It's also important to engage your teams when defining your metrics. So, follow the four critical areas for metrics that I shared in the Pillar 2 chapter, establish 1-2-3 key measures per area, and then iterate based on whether the measures are having a positive effect or not.

Ensure that you are listening attentively to your team along the way. In fact, each metric should be clearly understood by your whole organization and remember to keep things simple.

## *Testing Strategies*

There's a tremendous amount of bravado in the agile testing community that focuses on automated, unit, and story-based functional testing as the only testing that goes on within agile teams. The allusion is usually to 90% automation and to 10% of that other "pesky" testing stuff. Another allusion is that it's easy to achieve this balance.

However, these positions are unfortunately <u>wrong</u> in 90% of real world contexts.

As I mentioned earlier in the Pillar 2 chapter, agile testing is, at its core, a risk-based testing model. There are essentially three types of testing that you should carefully focus towards:

1. **Manual** – functional and non-functional testing (scripted);
2. **Automated** – functional and non-functional testing (using a multi-tiered model);
3. **Exploratory** testing (non-scripted)

Around all of these is a test design process that usually creates, or mines for, new tests from the manual and exploratory activity. Along with this process, the non-functional testing gets as much focus as the functional testing, with coverage of all major testing activities. For example: regression, system, integration, and user acceptance testing phases.

In my experience, there is typically a healthy balance between manual testing (25-40%), automated testing (50-60%), and exploratory testing techniques (15-20%), in mature agile organizations. It might take quite a bit of time to achieve it, but your longer-term strategy needs to be one of balance.

There is absolutely nothing wrong with focusing more on manual and exploratory testing in your early stages of agile transformation (if you lack an automation framework and automated tests).

## *Implications of Your Agile Release Train*

I want to remind you that there is a strong relationship between agile testing and your agile release tempo. Initially, you'll simply want to pick a release train tempo and explore the testing activity within it at various points:

- Pre-release train – Is your planning opportunity at a release level. This is where you'll look for testing "risks" to mitigate incrementally. It's where you'll define the amount of *Technical Test Debt* [20]you might incur and plan for mitigating it. It's where you'll define the high-level strategy for your hardening sprint(s) within the Release Trains. A key focus is for breadth of testing.

   If you're operating within a SAFe environment, then this would be part of your feature definition, backlog refinement, and ultimately PSI Planning events.

- Then, during each Sprint – Clearly, the focus here is on the sprint committed features and stories meeting the organizational and team DoD in all aspects. However, at the same time, previous work needs to be assured that it's still working. Quite often, notions of partial-integration and partial-regression testing are executed on a team-by-team basis.

- Then, during Hardening Sprint(s) – Hardening sprints are a place to "catch up" on your technical test debt with respect to coverage. If you've not run a full regression for a few sprints, and are concerned about regressions, then you might plan for running one. It's a place for increased non-functional testing work as well, although it should not preclude you from running non-functional tests during earlier sprints.

---

[20] Bob has written an article about the notion of Technical Debt as it applies to Quality and Testing activity. It broadens the definition beyond the code. You can find it here - http://rgalen.com/s/testingexperience18_06_18_Galen.pdf

- **During Release** – You'll want to agree on final testing activity and checklists that you'll run through. At iContact, we had a release night game plan for how we would be deploying and testing our product as we moved it fully into our production environment. There were checkpoints when it moved from environment to environment and as each were configured. Production level security and performance were also a key part of our testing and verification.

Of course, things will change based on each sprint's discovery and progress, but the overall strategy usually hangs together.

As they say, the plan wasn't that important, but the planning was priceless.

## *Wrapping Up*

This chapter is focused towards helping QA, Test Leaders, and Managers map their way forward into agile quality and testing while leveraging the Three Pillars framework. It's not intended to do it for you. Instead, I provided some thoughts around common and useful tactics.

Unfortunately (or fortunately), the "hard bits" will remain for you and your teams. But, I do hope this helps.

In the next and final chapter in the first edition, Mary Thorn will share on the QA Manager Role in Agile Organizations. I feel it nicely compliments and overlaps with this chapter. Between the two of them, I think we've armed you with sufficient ideas to get you moving forward in establishing, guiding, and accomplishing your agile quality and testing strategies.

## *References*

1. Salesforce was kind enough to share their Definition-of-Done at the 2010 Agile Conference. I've captures it in a slide deck I've used to share on various aspects of agile-centric release criteria. You can clearly Google for the Salesforce presentation. You can find mine here: http://rgalen.com/s/Agile-Release-Criteria-v5.pdf

2. Dean Leffingwell first mentions the Agile Release Train in his book Scaling Software Agility: Best Practices for Large Enterprises that he published in 2007. He later brought these ideas forward in his 2011 book on Agile Software Requirements and in the Scaled Agile Framework – SAFe. The Pillar 2 chapter discusses more details on the Agile Release Train.

# Chapter 6: Crossing Pillars:

# The Role of the QA Manager in Agile

Your first question might be – why does a QA Manager need a vision, strategy, or roadmap? Isn't that the role of the Product Owner? Or maybe even the Development Manager? But certainly not the QA Manager.

My question is if you don't have them, then what are you doing in a QA management or leadership role in the first place? Some people say that my primary job as a QA manager is people management. Granted, that is a big part of my job as it never goes away, not even in agile contexts, but it does not fully convey what I "do". When someone asks me what I do, I say – "I build high performing QA Teams". The next question I usually get is – "What does that mean?" My typical answer is – "I provide the vision, roadmap, and strategy for the QA team and remove any roadblocks that are impeding their success."

Bob asked me to add this chapter to the book from my point of view as an in-the-trenches QA and Testing leader. I wasn't too keen to do it, since I felt my "Mary's Corner" additions captured my experience. But he insisted. He felt that readers needed someone with real-world QA leadership role to explore things from a Three Pillars and agile perspective. He can be relatively persuasive, so here I go.

## Vision

When I talk about vision, I often think of my days as a collegiate basketball player when my coach would bring in sports psychologists. They would teach us how to envision winning the big game and what we could contribute to it, for example, by making the game-winning shot.

To be honest, I still do these exercises every day. I envision the things I could do to contribute more to my team's success and I envision all the things that need to happen to get us to the point of being high-performing. For those of you who are first time QA managers, you might not necessarily know what a high-performing QA team looks like, so you might challenge me to help you envision it.

**Characteristics of a high-performing QA team from my perspective include:**

- The QA team members are functioning as an equal part of the overall Agile and/or Scrum Organization. Within each team there is a healthy and respectful balance between "developers" and "testers". I see many agile implementations where the developers do their work in one sprint and then send that work to a separate team of testers to do system integration testing and regression in another sprint. This is inefficient and ineffective. Whole-team integration of the QA team members, as part of the actual Scrum teams is essential to delivering quality software.

- They are Subject Matter Experts (SMEs) in the area of the application domain. One of my favorite ways to recruit and hire QA candidates is to walk over to the Technical Support Manager, find the best person in their department, *and have them come to my QA team*[21]. The reason for this is these people have been on the phone for years talking to clients about what does not work for them. These support specialists are product-level SMEs who lack testing experience. Fortunately, testing can be taught and I've seen them consistently become outstanding testers.

- They are technically competent. Due to the adaptive nature of agile and delivering working software in fast iterative slices, testers do not have time for manual full regression testing every

---

[21] One of the side effects of using Exploratory Testing sessions and pairing at iContact, was that we would invite support engineers into the pairs. Because of their direct customer experience, they were "hot commodities" and very popular pair-mates. This also gave us both a chance to get to know each other and led to some very positive transfers.

sprint. Therefore automation becomes more important, and having testers who can code becomes essential. That does not mean that there are no longer manual testers, but my manual testers need to continuously become more technical. They need to be able to do complex SQL queries, or API testing, or any of the tests required for non-functional testing.

- The next five adjectives come from the book by Patrick Lencioni called "The Five Dysfunctions of a Team". The QA members are accountable, committed, trust their teammates, driven to results, and don't fear conflict. I've become a strong convert to the use of Five Dysfunctions in agile teaming contexts. You can reach out to Patrick's firm and engage them to do training and ongoing assessments. We did this at iContact and it provided great leadership insights into our teams strengths, weaknesses, and where we as leaders needed to focus our coaching.

- They are empowered to be change agents. Someone once asked me: "What is it that makes you successful?" My response was: "I am empowered to make change when necessary." This was all because I had a boss, a team, and a company that did not care what your title or hire date was. If you had a better way of improving the software or the process, just bring it up. While at times I think people might have wanted less frequent change, the company fully embraced it. It is essential for your QA team to be empowered to be change agents.

The bottom line is that you need to figure out what success looks like for your teams and create a vision of how to get there. To give you a quick example, at a firm where I've worked, there was a QA Manager who could not answer the questions from their manager as to how good the product quality was. They were consistently being asked for metrics around bugs, automation, and hours of manual testing vs. automated testing.

Their QA technical backlog was insufficient to be able produce this information for their boss and they were later removed as QA Manager. While I am not sure their boss really knew what the health of the product was either, he really just wanted to know what "good" was.

If the QA manager had had a vision of "good" and could have communicated it clearly, then I know that this demotion would have been avoided. And forget their boss; imagine working on this manager's team. How would you have liked coming to work every day and not knowing your direction?

## Roadmaps

Roadmaps are my favorite subject from January through March every year, as I am currently putting together my PowerPoint presentation for my boss and his boss around QA and our annual roadmap. The things that I have found helpful in having a QA roadmap include:

1) Transparency around areas where improvement is needed within QA, especially around areas of automation.
2) It helps define what success looks like for the QA personnel for the year, and it helps define individual objectives around this.
3) Defines the strategy discussed above.
4) It actually makes you look like you know what you are doing.

One of the more important parts of the roadmap is measurement. You need to determine goals, milestones, and then how you will measure success at each milestone. I much prefer negotiating this right up front, instead of waiting until the last minute. Literally, envision what success looks like and then ensure your leaders, both up and down, understand it.

## Who Creates Them?

I think there are three contributors to roadmaps:

1) Your team(s)
2) You as a leader (your experience, instincts, etc.)
3) Your organizational directives

## The TEAM

So where do you start? With – The Team, The Team, The Team, The Team and no that was not a typo.

I am sure some of you are saying – but I just said that it was part of the QA Manager's job. And it is, but the QA and Development team members should contribute all of the content. At a start-up company that I worked at, in my first week I put my QA team in a room and had a retrospective on how to get better as a team. This created the beginning of my strategic improvement product backlog. I then had them vote on their top five items and that influenced priority. Next I took all of the information from the retrospective and started to put the roadmap together.

Did I have personal influence and ideas for the backlog and subsequent roadmap? Of course I did. But I used the dynamics of team-based collaboration and problem-solving to help me craft an inclusive roadmap.

## You as a Leader

Once I understand what is important to the team, I then pull from my experience and add items that I know will make us successful. While I usually use my experience to get items on the board for discussion during the team retrospective, sometimes that does not happen and I make decisions to add additional roadmap items.

## Organizational Directives

Often there are organizational directives that influence the QA roadmap. For example, at a previous company they decided to start releasing software weekly. With that in mind, I knew that our automated tests had to run faster and give feedback quicker so that we could release whenever they wanted to. We had to add several roadmap items to be able to fulfill this goal.

Agile release train dynamics quite often influence the roadmaps within testing and quality organizations. It starts with your engagement in release planning, but it typically extends into execution beyond testing and into deployment and customer satisfaction.

## *Putting It All Together*

Once you have gathered all the input for your roadmap, put a baseline together. I say "baseline" because now you have to review it with key stakeholders to make sure they buy in to what you are trying to do. Every year, once I have my roadmap, I review it with my team again to make sure they agree.

I then review it with the product owners to make sure they understand the business value, and I review it with the development managers and their teams because it often affects how they work as well. Once we all agree to this, then I have my baseline roadmap for the year.

Socializing your roadmap cross-functionally is one of the most important things you can do for your teams. It makes your initiatives transparent across the organization and it allows them "cover" to support and operate under your plans. It should also be inclusive of other group commitments that are needed to support your efforts.

Point being – having a roadmap that has unsupported organizational dependencies is like having no roadmap at all. You need to continuously assure that the organization is aware of and fully supporting your efforts.

## What are examples of what would be in a typical roadmap?

Below are different items that I have included in my own QA roadmaps over the years:

- Build automation framework;
- Automate (n) smoke tests; tied to both future work and legacy technical debt;
- Automate (n) regression tests; tied to both future work and legacy technical debt;
- Define and/or implement performance testing strategy;
- Train for and/or implement BDD; keeping in mind that they is a testing team "part" to this and an organizational "part" as well;
- Train for and/or implement exploratory testing;
- Write manual regression test cases for (n) upcoming features in the Release Forecasts;
- Create QA Standard Operating Procedure documents;
- Migrate away from Quality Center/ALM and save the company $100k/year (BEST roadmap item ever)

As I've said, a key is to make them as clear, goal-oriented, and as measurable as possible.

If you're delivering to your goals in phases, and often I am, then you'll want to be clear about how items connect from one period of time to the next, for example quarterly.

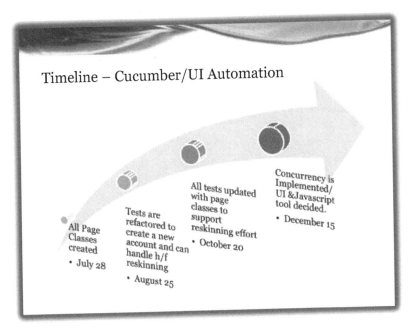

Figure 11, Sample Roadmap Slide

## *I Have One...Now What?*

Once you have your roadmap, you need to work with your Product Owner organization to create stories, and get them prioritized and injected across your organizational and individual team product backlogs. This is not always easy, as it often seems to undermine the product initiatives and direction. You will need to convince them of the importance of your work and how it fits into their overall strategies, roadmaps, and plans. Make sure that you put all of your work in a business context, explaining what it will do for them or the customer.

Another approach is to allocate a specific percentage of each backlog to this sort of work. While I was at iContact, we agreed on an allocation with Product Management that 20% of each team's backlog would be reserved for bug repair, refactoring, and infrastructure work. Our automation infrastructure efforts fell into this bucket and the preagreement made it much easier for me to negotiate our roadmap and deliver on automation.

Believe it or not, we often did not fill our 20% allocation, so we measured these items and became concerned when teams fell below a 10% allocation. It usually meant that product quality and our investments were off in some way. The usual root cause for this was a lack of effort or initiative within the teams. While they would often complain that things were not getting better, they would also not always give the effort needed to identify (and act on) improvement. Imagine that?

If you do not have a global agreement of some kind, you have to allocate your work to the Product Backlogs on a situation-by-situation basis. For example, at one of my past roles I was hired to create a QA department and to help implement agile across the organization. One of my biggest challenges was convincing Product Owners, who had never had QA members on their teams, that they needed to dedicate 10% of every sprint to helping create our automation framework and start writing and executing regression tests.

This process was frustratingly slow and painful. Luckily I had a Product Owner who eventually trusted what I was trying to do. After he saw value being created and bugs being found sprint by sprint, by the time I left he had upped his percentage of technical debt to 20%. Sometimes you just have to be persistent and show the value that effective QA and testing bring to the table from an overall product perspective.

## Roadmap – For Sale

Another thing that you will need to do is to "sell" the roadmap. You might ask – how do you sell a roadmap? Promote it in your next town hall, put it on your wiki, discuss it in agile meetings (for example: grooming, planning, retrospectives), email the group, talk about it in hallways, etc. This is actually one of the most critical steps in the process.

If you are not transparent about what you are trying to do, then nothing will ever get done. I cannot emphasize how important it is to keep it up-to-date and hold yourself and the team accountable to it. The worst thing you can do is get your team's hopes up that things are going to get better and then never follow through on it.

You should have continuous conversations around your roadmap – in hallways and in meetings. You can also leverage metrics in supporting your initiatives. You can introduce metrics into your yearly objectives or demonstrate items from them at your next sprint review. You can even put information radiators throughout your office displaying items of improvement from your roadmap. There are many ways to make your roadmap transparent – find out what works for you and make sure everyone knows what it is.

## Strategy

Strategy is defined as:

*A plan of action or policy designed to achieve a major or overall aim.*

Again, referencing my basketball roots, just like we envision hitting the game-winning shot, you have to come up with a strategy to put yourselves in a position to be able to take that shot. So what is your strategy as a QA Manager? Take the first item on your roadmap and start to make a plan of action to achieve it. It's that simple.

For example, at a financial firm where I once worked, they were almost through their transition from traditional waterfall testing to agile testing. Being a regulated financial firm, trying to understand what waterfall documentation is truly required for audits in an agile context had been difficult to cross-reference. When I was hired, I came up with a strategy of being able to move fast within the agile context but still do the testing and documentation that was required for the regulatory requirements. To do this I had to determine what the minimum test standards were. For us they were pretty simple:

1) Document what you think you need to test
2) Document the tests for the above
3) Prove that you ran the test
4) Ensure results are documented and stored

Then I had figure out all the test phases that where required across Functional QA, Integration, UAT, and Production. Once I had all known requirements, the team came together and mapped out an agile testing strategy that would meet all standards. In our case, we easily mapped this to our Agile Release Train tempo.

The key here, though, is executing the strategy once you have one. The team has to get it done, do it incrementally, measure it, and make adjustments along the way. With that said, I cannot emphasize enough how much you should collaborate with your team in the execution phase. This will allow them to buy into the strategy and help contribute in terms of how they think the strategy should be executed. It also gives them ownership and accountability, while creating trust. Without team buy-in and the QA Manager's leadership of the strategy, it is worth no more than writing on a piece of paper.

## Closed Loop

Please keep in mind that although I serially described:

- Vision
- Roadmap
- Strategy

As the sequence of events for leading your initiatives and teams, please don't view them as a series of events in a project plan. Instead, they all occur in parallel and feedback into one another as you move forward. You'll want to have a view towards continuous improvement, learning, and adjustment across all of your plans. In fact, it's this ability to monitor the landscape and make fine-tuning adjustments based on the reality on the ground that separates the good from great leaders. And don't forget to listen to your team constantly as they're executing.

## Leadership Examples

I thought it would be helpful, well Bob is actually making me do this part, to share some of my experiences as it relates to this chapters' theme and the Three Pillars. I'll share three examples as a way of hopefully adding additional context in illustrating effective management and leadership within agile contexts.

## *Example 1*

*When I was interviewing for the job at iContact my first interview (in this case coffee) with Bob we discussed Agile and the roles in Scrum. Having only 2-3 years of agile experience under my belt and I had only recently received my CSM I felt very intimidated by this man with 10-15 years of experience building agile teams.*

*We discussed their problems with automation and how their first try was unsuccessful, and how the QA manager that came in would need to work with the new framework that was being built and re-target it to be faster to write tests and more scalable. I said to him sounds like your asking me to be the Product Owner for the automation team. At that point Bob's face lit up, I could tell he had never thought of it that way, and I knew I had at least a 2nd interview.*

*Fast forward to when I was hired and had a month of tenure. I had realized that the new open source framework that they were implementing (Cucumber) was great at writing tests fast but unfortunately the tests were fragile. Fragile in the sense that sometimes the test passed in CI and sometimes they did not. The root cause was that the team had not used any OOO design patterns like Page Objects so if a menu label changed they would have to refactor 100 tests. They had also implemented a headless open source browser because in theory that should be faster than a headed browser. Lastly the team had several different opinions on how to fix these problems.*

*So one day I pulled them all in a room, along with the CI team, and a few rogue developers who had taken a liking to the Cucumber framework. We spent an hour brainstorming our goals, challenges, and discussing all the different things we wanted to change. We then spent another hour prioritizing the list based on the greatest return on investment. From that moment on I played the role of Product Owner and QA Manager. I entered all the stories in Jira, we had active backlog refinement meetings, we did sprint planning, and conducted daily standups. I created a quarterly roadmap that I would present at our monthly Town Hall Meetings and also provided the vision of where we wanted the framework to go.*

One thing I have failed to mention here is, during this time I told Bob that we had to stop creating tests. This was slightly unfavorable to him because we had spent the previous six months building a selenium framework that only produced 16 tests, and they had been on Cucumber for a month and already had close to 300 written. He thought that we could continue to write tests and work on the framework at the same time. After pleading my case that the 300 were so fragile that if we add to it the technical debt would take to long to over come, he understood and gave us the "space" to refactor our framework.

Over the next three months we got through the blocking stories and solidified the framework to the point where we could go back to writing tests. I played Product Owner for three more months until the point where we had built a pretty amazing framework. Now when our tests failed it was mostly due to bugs.

As we accelerated through automating our regression test cases, we were able to significantly reduce the length of our hardening sprint. At this point I disbanded the automation team and moved the development and support of all automation into the Scrum teams so they could start automation sprint work within our normal product release tempo.

## Example 2

I come from a life of working at startup companies. All in all, I have worked in six different startups from where I usually had to hire and unfortunately a lot of times fire most of my QA team. With each different startup there were always challenges, mostly never enough people to do the work or a lack of testing infrastructure. So when I walked into iContact I felt that I had hit the jackpot as far as having a ratio of 1:2.5 testers to developers on each Scrum team.

They truly understood that testing was craft and that testers brought value to their Scrum teams. There was something here that mattered more than anywhere else, the actual Scrum team itself. The teams were so empowered that they would "vote team members off the island" if they were not holding their weight or dragging down the team. Within the first month I found myself in a predicament where one of my testers was being let go due to "Voted Off". Bob and I discussed this several times over the next year and the characteristics of the people I needed to hire so they would fit in to our test infested teams. We made sure that were hired *people that where great communicators, had positive attitudes, and loved collaboratively working in teams.*

*Over the next year the skillsets and the personalities changed. When I first got there I had an automation team with two guys working on a framework. I had five contractors and five fulltime staff members with 80% of those as manual testers and 20% automation focused. So to be clear I had two testers on each five Scrum teams and two automation guys off to the side building frameworks. As in the previous story you can see how automation started to play a huge role as we figured out how we could leverage automation on the Scrum teams.*

*Over that year what we found out that worked best for us was to have one manual tester and one automation developer on each Scrum team. We had several testers that did not want to do automation but were valuable and we had several automation developers that did not want to do manual testing. So once the framework was built we moved the automation guys into the Scrum teams, we let a few of the contractors go and ended up with the right combination of skillsets and personalities. Just for reference, if I get to build a team from scratch I want the testers to do both manual and automation testing, and not have those roles split. But in this case most of the team already existed and I worked with what I had.*

*You might wonder who kept of the framework once the automation guys got in the teams. The answer is the teams did. The whole-team owned quality and if they saw that the framework needed repair, a story was written, put on the backlog and prioritized accordingly. I am not a big fan of splitting off an automation team where you test the code in a sprint and the next sprint a separate group automates it. You create a lot of churn and technical test debt that way. Specifically a developer is not going to want to go back and put Id's on buttons or fix a bug a sprint later when it should have happened during the sprint.*

*Over the past seven years working in agile environment I have found that ratios matter. That I have to hire on:*

1. *Attitude first*
2. *Then Aptitude*
3. *And then Skillset*

*in that order [22]with no exceptions.*

*I've also learned that I also have to hire team players that are great communicators and collaborators. Players who are comfortable working within a team structure where they might not have the same skills as others, yet still need to work together. I have also debated the concept of specialists versus generalists in agile teams. While I try to hire testers that are more generalist in nature, I however still believe that software testing is a craft and that QA Engineers still provide major value to their Scrum teams.*

## *Example 3*

*After Bob introduced me to the Three Pillars, I've started to consistently use it as my report card to drive my roadmaps and testing strategies. At a more recent company I worked at, I walked into a very agile company but with no vision or strategy of what good agile testing looks like. I spent my first week on the job talking with the development managers, the second week talking to the testers on my team, and the third week with the Product Owners discussing what current issue they had with my test team.*

*In the fourth week, I took all the results and made a State of QA presentation to my boss and peers. The goal was to get team-based input from all sides and not assume I knew what the problems were. At the end of the presentation I displayed the Three Pillars, to establish a baseline of where my strategies would be going. I had spent the previous 45 minutes discussing all the bad things, but I still needed to educate them on what my forward looking vision was as we addressed the issues.  Interestingly,*

---

[22] To give full credit, this idea came from Ralph Kasuba, our CTO while at iContact. Ralph would reiterate these three attributes AND the priority order constantly in our hiring planning and discussions. He would actually "quiz" us on them. But all joking aside, having this sort of leadership vision for recruiting and team skill focus is incredibly valuable when building high-performance agile teams.

*all the issues I had to fix could be addressed if I simply implemented the Three Pillars strategy.*

*When I was in the interview process I asked the question "Why are you hiring for this position", what does "good" look like? For this company it was reduce the amount of post release defects and have more consistency across QA. This feedback allowed me set that goal for my QA team.*
*You might ask which pieces of the Three Pillars did I implement first? Like Bob mentions, you have to be balanced across all Three Pillars, therefore I strategically chose one item from each pillar to address for the first quarter.*

*My roadmap for Q1 consisted of: from Pillar 1 to finalize our automation strategy and tool, from Pillar 2 Standards and templates, and Pillar 3 create doneness criteria. For Quarter 2 my roadmap consisted of: implementing our new automation framework and set it up in CI from Pillar 1, implement risk-based test planning from Pillar 2, and code reviews and standards from Pillar 3.*

*After Q2 I decided to have a QA retrospective to see if any of the original problems had been improved or resolved and/or what new issues have arisen since I started. I also discussed with the development managers and Product Owners whether they saw improvement. The good news is that people did see improvement, while not perfect testing was being perceived as better.*

*I try to do these retrospectives at least every six months to ensure the problems I perceive we fixed or improved actually are. The retrospective also helped me decide what to put on my roadmap for Q3 and Q4 and what areas of the Three Pillars to work on next.*

*You might ask – did I achieve the goal of reduced number of customer defects post release and QA consistency using the Three Pillars? Yes, the testers on the team used the same process and had the same deliverables so that if you had to move a tester from one Scrum team to another you could. Our post release defects were better but not great because implementing the Three Pillars and process improvement in general takes time. As I mentioned to by boss in the interview process you won't see earth-shattering improvements in quality for 12-18 months. I do know however that things were getting better, more consistent, and were on the right track by following the Three Pillars approach.*

## *Wrapping Up*

So, is the above a "slam dunk" to win the game? No. But someone once asked me: "What are the three great characteristics of a Product Owner?" and I responded:

1) They understand their business context;
2) They have a strategy, vision, and roadmap and can effectively communicate them;
3) They are organized.

To be honest, I feel like these are exactly the same three characteristics needed to be a good QA Manager. If you do these three things then you should be able to at least set up the team to "win" the race.

# Afterthoughts

## From Bob

This is the first book that I've completed by partnering with someone else. Yes, I've had many reviewers, but never working with someone as close as I have with Mary. In short, I liked it. I have a tendency to write at a higher, strategic level and sometimes readers have trouble envisioning how to take my stories, points, recommendations, and guidance down to a real world level.

I think Mary has helped with that connection and the book is better for it. I want to sincerely thank her for her interest, time, and perspective.

### *Please Stay Context-Focused*

Jurgen Appelo makes a general point in his Management 3.0 book that all models and frameworks are essentially flawed or broken; every one of them. I wholeheartedly agree with him. But the other side of the point is that – some of them are actually useful.

And the usefulness is within targeted contexts. So please don't take the Three Pillars model or any of our recommendations, stories, and tactics too seriously. They're intended to get you to think. To apply them, with your and your teams' experience, to your own contexts and to use what is...USEFUL.

Throw away or ignore the rest. And I hope you found some value in the book.

And here's a request from TR Buskirk, one of the early reviewers, that nicely compliments this section:

*One silly request: If you could add this line in the book somewhere, it would help arm those of us with experience defend ourselves from people who find something in a book and use it as holy writ:*

*"Testers who worked with Bob or Mary can quote this line of the book to prove their argument is correct if the only competing argument is also a random citation"*

Thanks TR! Stay agile my friends...

## From Mary

When Bob and I started to discuss writing this book, I was all in. I was passionate about the need for a book like this and thought that Bob and I could fill the void. Truth be told writing a book is hard. Truth be told Bob is amazing with words and I, well let's just say I am grammatically challenged. I once had a Product Owner say to me "Mary you're one of the best testers I have ever worked with but you cannot spell worth a damn". I thank Bob for the continued guidance and pushing me to get things written, reviewed, rewritten, rewritten again, and well you get the point.

I hope that the framework is as successful for you as I feel it has been for me. To Bob's point, there are things that will not always work for you but I promise you there are things in it that will. I don't have a slogan like Bob that he ends his emails and books with as in "Stay agile my friend". I will though wish you luck in your agile testing transition!

## *Coming Attractions*

As I said in the Introduction, we're planning on publishing more information around the Three Pillars, but not necessarily all in another edition of the book.

What we envision are:

- A Leanpub version of the book, which will be our "vehicle" for providing iterative content after the first edition. Leanpub has a wonderful platform for providing iterative updates in a variety of e-formats. www.leanpub.com
  - We'll also be leveraging Leanpub for Apple iBook format releases
- We'll be writing our ideas in blog posts and articles. We keep a
- We'll be leveraging blog posts as a way for you to interact on the Three Pillars framework.
- We'll be making Three Pillars Assessment worksheet available on my website – along with updating it as we fine-tune it and adjust to your feedback.
- And finally, we'll be making PDF copies of our additional topic Deep Dives available on the website (as well as Leanpub).

So it's probably worth your while to join our 3-Pillars mailing list here:

http://goo.gl/ORcxbE

# Appendix A

# Three Pillars Assessment Framework

One of the final things that made sense to include in the book was a means of evaluating your application and support of the Three Pillars across your organization and teams. To that end, Mary and I have pulled together an assessment spreadsheet for you to use.

Before we get into it, we want to be clear. We both DO NOT like agile assessments and scorecards in general. Why? Because they can be misused and ultimately become destructive to your agile culture, teams, and journey.

With that being said though, it's really hard to leverage the Three Pillars without some sort of tool.

## *Disclaimer*

1.  You promise to only use the tool as a device to positively guide your agile journey.
2.  You promise to leverage the tool as a means of achieving and staying in balance across your agile quality and testing practices.
3.  You promise never to use it to measure individuals or teams – meting out performance evaluations, merit increases, bonuses, or other such "management stuff".
4.  You promise to use it as a baseline, share with your team(s) and iteratively change what you assess/measure as you mature in your Three Pillars journey.

## *Assessment Tool*

You can gain access to the tool here – http://goo.gl/Q77on8

Below are the primary assessment areas for the tool. You'll notice that we've created five core questions for each of the three pillars and the foundational elements. We've also included a leadership assessment area, mostly because we feel that effective leadership and alignment is required for ultimate success in improving your agile quality and testing.

| Development and Test Automation Pillar |
| --- |
| Pyramid -based test automation infrastructure is in place and automated tests are being created at the unit, integration and UI levels. |
| Continuous Integration/Deployment infrastructure is in place and ALL automated tests run as part of your CI/CD processes. You also couple your CI/CD infrastructure to your DevOps environments and to your Automation Architecture. |
| Test automation-centric technical debt is being actively scheduled and reduced. This would be at a pyramid-level basis and also include automation infrastructure. |
| Actively practicing ATDD, BDD and letting "acceptance tests" guide your feature development. You started this effort with "manual" user story writing and acceptance test execution, so that you have the basics down. |
| Visual feedback radiators (dashboards, lights, alarms, lava lamps, etc.) are setup to view build and test runs. Developers and testers monitor these radiators and take immediate action when builds or tests fail. |

## Software Testing Pillar

Test planning occurs at the Release and Sprint planning levels. If you're using a release train, you've coupled test planning to Release Train - PSI Planning events.

Risk based testing is utilized to reduce scope of testing work and clearly indicates what the tester IS and IS NOT testing in the sprint. Testing focus changes day-to-day and sprint-to-sprint.

Exploratory Testing sessions (SBET, preferably paired) are a regular part of your sprint and release tempos. Charters are actively kept up-to-date, de-briefs are held, and pairing is leveraged. It's a whole-team activity.

As a tester you have consistent standards, templates and checklists that are used across every team. You have a repository that makes ALL artifacts transparent. And your development colleagues can openly contribute to all of this.

Testing is balanced across manual, exploratory and automated testing; including functional and non-functional tests, with each team determining the effective ratio across approaches.

## Cross Functional Team Pillar

Team based pairings are a natural part of everyday collaboration between testers, developers, and PO. In other words, active 3-Amigos discussions are continuous.

When the build or test run fails, appropriate team members drop what they are working on and fix the issues. Stop-the-line behavior is clearly exhibited whenever and wherever appropriate.

Code reviews occur for everything (application code, automation, scripts) that are checked in by developer's or testers. It's a strong part of the culture and Definition-of-Done.

There is a multi-tiered Definition-of-Done in place: team member work product-level, user story-level, sprint-level, and release-level and teams adhere to the DoD. It also comes into play in story estimation.

Testers are part of grooming, design, and any requirement meeting when there is a developer and PO involved in the conversation. And they are active contributors.

## Whole Team Ownership

Stories are iterated through the sprint with multiple development-testing cycles (e.g. the sprint is not a waterfall OR no Scrummerfall allowed). Swarming occurs naturally and often.

Analysts/developers and testers collaborate on building test plans. More than that, the entire team contributes to iterative testing strategies towards release goals.

Entire team is aware of, talks about and communicates technical debt and technical test debt. They also actively "manage" it via work in the Product Backlog.

The team owns the responsibility for requirements and everything that ensues from them — code, testing, functionality, satisfaction levels, etc. There is also continuous customer engagement.

When automated tests fail, any person on the team takes the initiative to fix the failed test, not just the "testers" on the team. If any team member has the technical ability, they feel like they can create / maintain any automated test.

## Test Leadership

Managers are routinely involved in improving test practice and implementing best practices, not by pushing, but by influence and engagement with the team. Being "pulled" into helping guide improvements.

Managers are routinely part of the release-level or PSI planning with their teams. They help guide effective risk and x-team dependency management. They are also part of sprint/release go/no go decision-making.

There is a dedicated practice center of excellence that is dedicated to building automation libraries, standardize measures for quality, and perform coaching and mentoring for testing professionals.

A clear Testing Roadmap is established that is published/ presented at least 2x a year. Progress is being steadily and transparently made against the roadmap.

Test managers actively participate in steering Agile evolution organizationally and across teams. They naturally partner with their development colleagues.

# Index